THE MAGNA ILLUSTRATED GUIDE TO
CATS
OF THE WORLD

About the author
Howard Loxton, author of a number of books on cats and cat care, lives in London with a pair of Siamese. He was adopted by a coal-black kitten in the middle of the blitz and has been a devoted felinophile ever since.

About the artist
Peter Warner, artist, print maker and illustrator, was trained at the Royal Academy Schools. He is particularly well known for his animal and natural-history studies, often sketched from life near his home in the Kent countryside. His Seal Point Siamese and three mongrel cats have frequently posed as models.

THE MAGNA ILLUSTRATED GUIDE TO
CATS
OF THE WORLD

Howard Loxton

Illustrations by Peter Warner

MAGNA BOOKS

Acknowledgements

The author, artist and publishers would like to express their thanks to the many breeders and cat owners who have helped in the preparation of this volume. In particular they wish to express their indebtedness to the Governing Council of the Cat Fancy for giving permission to quote from their official Standards for the various breeds, to Mrs Grace Pond to whose many books any present day writer on cats must owe a considerable debt and through whose kindness contact was established with a number of American breeders; to Mrs Anne Cumbers whose fine photographs provided an invaluable reference source to complement the artist's studies from life; to Dr Frank Manolson for an inexhaustable supply of veterinary knowledge and to Mme Stephe Bruin for her watchful eye and expert advice throughout.

Special thanks is also due to Mrs Blanche V. Smith, Breed Editor of *Cats Magazine* and Mr Patrick L. Oliver, Mrs Grace M. Clute of the Cat Fancier's Federation, Mrs Fern Husky of the American Cat Fanciers Association, the Cat Fanciers' Association Inc, and to the following for advising on the breeds in which they specialize: Mrs Nancy Lane of Newcastle, Delaware (Exotic Short-hairs); Ms Gisela Stoscheck of Van Etten, New York (Angoras); Ms Ann Baker, of Riverside, Carolina (Ragdolls); Mrs Carolyn McLaughlin of Chicago (Japanese Bobtails); Mr and Mrs Harry Mague of Gillette, New Jersey (Somalis), Miss S. Birch of Hove (Balinese), Mrs Nancy Hilleard and Miss Barbara Stock (Rex). Mrs Margaret Manolson, Mrs J. Pruce, Miss Lydia Segrave and Mr and Mrs Ted Wilding also gave invaluable help.

First published in Great Britain by Elsevier Phaidon
(an imprint of Phaidon Press Limited)

© 1975 Andromeda Oxford Ltd

This edition published in 1993 by Magna Books
Magna Road
Leicester LE18 4ZH

ISBN 1 85422 426 3

Printed in Singapore

CONTENTS

THE CAT FAMILY

The first members of the cat family evolved 8 to 10 million years ago, long before the appearance of man. Palaeontologists describe a weasel-like, carnivorous animal which they called *Miacis*. It lived about 50 million years ago, had a long body and short legs and was probably the ancestor of the dog and of the bear as well as the predecessor of the cat.

Ten million years later one branch of its descendants had evolved into the first cat-like carnivore (it was another 10 million years before the first dog appeared) and eventually there emerged the whole range of animals which we know as the cat family. The first cat of 40 million years ago was an Old World animal which must have been extremely well-suited to its environment, for it remained relatively unchanged at a time when other mammals were developing rapidly. Known to us as *Dinictis*, it was about the same size as a lynx and looked very like modern cats; its canine teeth, however, were much larger and its brain was much smaller.

The descendants of *Dinictis* seem to have branched in two directions. In some the canine teeth became even larger. This group includes the genus *Machairodus*, or sabre-toothed cats, and it is possible that *Dinictis* should really be classed as one of them and that there was an early common ancestor for this and the other later cats. The second group had smaller canine teeth and included the Felidae, the family to which all modern cats belong.

At Rancho La Brea in southern California, close to Los Angeles, is a group of asphalt pits from which many examples of prehistoric big cats have been recovered. In Pleistocene times there were water pools lying on top of the pools of tar which oozed from beneath the ground. Small animals which came to drink were often trapped in the tar which, as it dried, became like a huge sheet of tacky fly-paper. Old or injured carnivores, or young and inexperienced ones, who thought that they had found some easy prey in the small animals caught in it, were themselves stuck fast and their bones preserved in the asphalt. The North American species, *Smilodon californicus*, one of the most advanced sabre-tooths, has been found in the greatest numbers. The long canine teeth which curved beyond the lower jaw when the mouth was closed were used not to bite prey but to deliver a violent stabbing blow. Also found at Rancho La Brea, although in only about one-thirtieth the number, perhaps because it was more intelligent, are the remains of the *Felis atrox* or "American Lion". This was a close relation of the European Cave Lion which survived until the 5th century BC when some of them are said to have attacked the baggage train of Xerxes when his army invaded Macedonia. The last dated Californian *Smilodon* lived about 13,000 years ago but the sabre-tooths disappeared from Europe very much earlier.

The sabre-tooths were adapted to hunt animals like the mammoths and mastodons who relied chiefly on their size and thick hide for their protection but had little defence against the sabre-tooths' stabbing teeth. When these giant land mammals died out the highly-specialized big cat also disappeared. It is from the less-specialized descendants of *Dinictis*, the Felidae, that the 36 species of cats we know today have developed.

The Living Genera

The members of the cat family have adapted and diversified to fit a wide range of climates and environments but they are all carnivores and are lithe and efficient hunters. Some are solitary; others, the lions in particular, often live in large groups. They range considerably in size — from the massive tiger to the 4½-lb Flat-headed Cat. In the past, the cat family has been divided into various different genera, but recent research into extinct forms suggests that the differences between them have little significance and many authorities now group them in the same genus with just one exception, the Cheetah, which is placed in a genus of its own, *Acinonyx*, because it is distinct from the other cats in a number of ways, among them that its claws do not retract. The big cats (once considered a separate genus, *Panthera*) can roar, while the smaller ones have higher-pitched voices; they have to take a breath between each purr, while the small cats can purr almost continuously; and they have larger heads in proportion to their bodies.

The Lion (*Felis leo*) is the strongest of the cats. The long body rests on short legs and is powerfully muscled. Unlike other cats most male lions have a luxuriant mane covering the head and shoulders and continuing as a fringe

Smilodon californicus *in the Rancho La Brea tar pools*

under the belly. It may be silvery blond or all shades through reddish brown to black and is not fully grown until the lion is about five years old. Females, who have no mane, are also smaller and lighter in build but it is they who most frequently make the kill when hunting. Lions are sociable animals and live in a family-based pride consisting of an older male, several females, adolescent males, and cubs which will usually number about 8 but may be as many as 30 where there is open terrain with plentiful prey. Their hunting is often carefully planned with one party chasing a herd of herbivores into an ambush formed by the rest of the pride lying upwind. Lion cubs are born with spotted markings which fade as they mature although they may persist in adulthood, particularly in lionesses. They begin to be weaned at about eight weeks but are not able to catch their own prey until they are about two years old. Because they are the last in the pride to eat, many cubs die in these early years.

Lions once ranged across much of Europe, Africa and western Asia but are now limited to central Africa, the Kruger National Park in South Africa and the Gir forest sanctuary in north-west India which is the only place where the Asiatic Lion is now known to survive.

The Tiger (*Felis tigris*) ranges from central Asia and north-eastern China through Malaya and India to parts of Persia and as far south as Bali. The Siberian Tiger, long-haired and the largest of its species, may measure over 13 ft from nose to tip of tail but the average tiger, like the average lion, is probably just under 9 ft overall. They usually lead a solitary life – although there have been reports of tigers hunting in pairs – and are mainly nocturnal. Litters usually consist of two to four cubs, although there may be more, and the young follow their mother hunting when they are only five weeks or so old. As they get older the area in which they hunt extends and the cubs play an increasingly large role in the kill until the family splits up when they are two to three years old.

Markings vary considerably from animal to animal and an unusual form of white tiger has occasionally occurred. This is not an albino but is an "extreme dilute": the ground colour is cream marked with light grey or brown stripes; the pads and nose leather are pink and the eyes are ice-blue.

The Leopard (*Felis pardus*) is the third largest of the big cats, averaging about 7½ ft from nose to tail tip. With the exception of the domestic cat they have a wider geographical distribution than any other member of the cat family, ranging through most of Africa south of the Sahara, across Asia from Arabia and the Caucasus to China and Korea and into Indonesia. They usually hunt alone although groups of up to six have been reported. Where hunted by man they are almost entirely nocturnal but elsewhere may be seen in early morning and late evening. They are good climbers and their spotted fur provides an excellent camouflage among dappled leaves. In the case of the black or melanistic variety, commonly known as the panther, the spots can still be distinguished in certain lights. When hunting they will often lie on a tree branch waiting to drop on prey beneath and then carry their kill – which can be as large as themselves – up into the tree, lodging it in a fork out of the reach of thieves. When prey is plentiful, as for instance

African Lion

Tiger

Leopard

during the migrations of the wildebeest, they will build up a well-stocked larder. There are usually three cubs in a litter but their survival rate is low and the number of leopards is declining.

The Snow Leopard (*Felis uncia*), or Ounce, is a closely related species which lives near the snow line and has a thick coat to protect it from the cold. It inhabits the sparsely-populated mountain regions of Asia from the Hindu Kush across Tibet into the Tsinghai and Szechwan provinces of China and the Altai mountains. Hunting at night or in late evening it preys on wild goats, sheep, deer, Persian gazelle and small mammals which live in the rocky grasslands between the tree line and the snow line and in summer ranges to pastures 13,000 ft above sea level. Litters of two or four are born in the spring and stay with their mothers until they are about a year old.

The Jaguar (*Felis onca*) is the only surviving big cat in the New World. It ranges from southern California, Arizona and the Gulf of Mexico south as far as the pampas of Argentina and the Rio Negro, and its territory seems limited more by the availability of prey than by climate or terrain, for it is found both in the high Andes and in mangrove swamps. It is usually a solitary hunter, although gregarious at breeding time when groups of eight or more have been seen. It is a good climber and a strong swimmer. As well as deer, agoutis, tapirs, peccaries, capybara and tree-living animals like monkeys, it also catches fish, turtles and small alligators and crocodiles.

The Clouded Leopard (*Felis nebulosa*) is the largest of all the Asian purring cats. It is a great climber and is found in really thick jungles where it remains concealed in the branches during the day and hunts at night. Ranging from Nepal across to China and Taiwan and south to Java, it may be as small as 2 ft in body length to $3\frac{1}{2}$ ft, plus 3 ft of tail. They are presumed to prey on small mammals but are rarely seen and little is known of their hunting or breeding habits.

The Cheetah (*Acinonyx jubatus*), which is placed in a separate genus, differs from all other members of the cat family in that its claws are not retractile after the age of about 10 weeks. It shares with the smaller cats the vocal apparatus which enables it to purr continuously but it lies down with its paws stretched out in front of it like the big cats, whereas the smaller cats usually tuck theirs in. It also hunts by day running its prey down instead of stalking it for it is reputedly the fastest four-legged animal in the world and has little to fear from predators. It is claimed that Cheetahs can accelerate to 45 mph in only two seconds and over short distances they can reach speeds of over 60 mph.

Cheetahs used to range right across North Africa and through Iran and Afghanistan to India and southward through Africa. Such areas provided open country where they could put their speed to advantage with enough grass to feed their prey and sufficient bushes to give them a little cover when hunting. They now survive only in a few places in Asia; in many parts of Africa, especially the north, they have also become quite rare. The adult Cheetah is about $4\frac{1}{2}$ ft long plus another $2\frac{1}{2}$ ft of tail. The head is small with less powerful jaws than those of the big cats but its light, lithe build incorporates a well-muscled neck, loins and limbs. Cubs, born in litters of two

Snow Leopard

Clouded Leopard

Jaguar

11

to four, have long woolly fur of smoke grey with a silver mane running down their backs. At about ten weeks of age the adult coat, which has a ground colour of reddish yellow broken by spots of solid black, begins to develop. In ancient and modern times cheetahs have been trained to hunt like coursing hounds.

The Puma (*Felis concolor*), also known as the Cougar and the Mountain Lion, ranges right through the Americas from British Columbia to Tierra del Fuego. It can be found in deserts, plains, mountains, and forests (though not commonly in the equatorial forests) and there are at least 15 different races, the larger of which live in the cooler climates and the smaller in the tropics. A large male might measure 5 ft plus a further 3 ft of tail, making it the largest member of the "small" cat group. The larger animals take large prey, especially deer, but have rarely been known to attack man for they are very cautious and have retreated from civilization's advance across the continent. The coat may vary from a light brown to black and the kittens are born with a black ringed tail and heavy spotting which fade as they grow up. The young usually stay with their mother until they are two years old and, although siblings sometimes stay together for a short time longer, the adult Puma leads a solitary life.

The Lynx (*Felis lynx*) is the only cat which is native to both the Old and the New World. Of medium size, about 3 to $3\frac{1}{2}$ ft long plus a tail of 5 to 8 in, its coat ranges from a sandy grey to a tawny red with white underparts. In summer the fur is thin and spotted with black but in winter it becomes dense and softer and the spots usually disappear. The North American Lynx is usually bigger with longer fur that is sometimes almost white. The ears have long black tufts and there is a ruff of long hair on the cheeks which stands up when they hiss in anger. It once lived right through the temperate forest belt of the Northern Hemisphere but the advance of man has now forced it into more remote regions. It is an expert jumper and climber and will hunt by day away from men but only at night when in their vicinity.

The Bobcat (*Felis rufa*) ranges from southern Canada south to southern Mexico but is not found in the corn belt of the Mid-West. Smaller than the lynx it replaces it in warmer regions and lives in more open ground. Although hunted by man both for its fur and for sport, its size and adaptability have helped it to survive. Its markings are more like those of the European Lynx but its tail tends to be longer and its ear tufts shorter. Male Bobcats help to raise the litter of up to four kittens but are not allowed near them until they have been weaned.

The Caracal (*Felis caracal*), has tufted ears and a short tail like the lynx and replaces it in warmer territories of the Old World ranging from the desert lands of the southern USSR, northern India and the Middle East to much of Africa. It likes open, mountainous or thinly-bushed country and keeps away from forests. It can survive in semi-desert conditions but is becoming scarce in much of its range, especially in Asia. Kittens are at first reddish brown but then grow silvery hairs which make them more grey than their mother. When adult they are the most powerful of the smaller African cats and can leap high into the air, even catching birds in flight.

Cheetah

Lynx

Bobcat

Puma

13

The Serval (*Felis serval*) inhabits open savannahs over a wide area of Africa south of the Sahara. It shows some resemblance to the lynx and caracal but its huge ears, which provide acuity of hearing beyond that of other cats, are set close together and have no ear tufts and its tawny coat is marked with black spots. It grows to about 3 ft long plus about 1 ft of tail.

The Sand Cat (*Felis margarita*) is another cat with big widely-spaced ears. About the size of the domestic cat, it lives in semi-desert areas of North Africa and the Middle East. It is seldom seen but its tracks are easily identified because its foot pads are almost covered with fur.

Another small African cat about which little is known because it is so rare is the Black-Footed Cat (*Felis nigripes*), named for the colour of the underside of its feet. Its range is limited to the Kalahari Desert, the western part of Orange Free State and parts of Botswana. It is slightly smaller than the domestic cat but has been known to cross-breed with it.

The African Golden Cat (*Felis aurata*) lives on the fringes of forests in West Africa, on the edge of the Guinea savannah and sometimes high in mountains. Although it owes its name to its lustrous golden-brown coat some individuals have a grey-blue colouring. When adult it is about $2\frac{1}{2}$ ft long plus half as much again of tail.

The Jungle Cat (*Felis chaus*) is somewhat larger than the other small African cats and ranges from Egypt across Asia to India, the Caucasus and Vietnam. It likes low marshy ground with plenty of cover so has also gained the name of Swamp Cat. It is a grizzled fawn with black stripes on the legs and near the end of the tail and some indistinct spotting on the body. The ears have black tufts but less developed than in the lynx and caracal.

The African Wild Cat (*Felis lybyca*) is slightly larger than the average domestic cat and ranges through all types of savannah in Africa and in south-west Asia. It prefers lightly forested country and is largely nocturnal although it may be seen about on cool days. There is a wide variation of colour but the whole coat is marked like the domestic tabby. Although a nocturnal hunter which usually remains hidden during the day this species can be tamed and can breed with the domestic cat.

The European Wild Cat (*Felis sylvestris*) actually ranges from Britain through Europe into Western Asia. Once quite common throughout wooded territory (except in Ireland) it has now retreated to remote areas away from man. It is difficult to distinguish one from a large domestic tabby that has gone feral but in fact they have larger skulls and teeth and the tip of the tail is rounded rather than pointed. They hunt nocturnally for birds and rodents but will also eat beetles and grasshoppers and on the west coast of Scotland have learned to fish.

The Ocelot (*Felis pardalis*) sometimes occurs in the southern United States and is common through Central and South America as far south as Paraguay. Four feet long in the body plus 15 in of tail it swims well and is an excellent climber. Where it is undisturbed by man it is diurnal but its beautiful fur has been much sought after and it is now largely a nocturnal animal hunting, sometimes in pairs, on the forest floor and sometimes taking birds or small mammals in trees and reptiles which include one record

Ocelot

Caracal

Temminck's Golden Cat

Flat-headed Cat

European Wild Cat

Jaguarondi

15

of a 7-ft boa-constrictor. There are believed to be two breeding seasons in the year.

The Margay (*Felis wiedi*) is very like the Ocelot and closely related to it but is considerably smaller: about 2 ft long plus a foot or more of tail. Distribution is similar to that of the Ocelot but fewer occur in the United States and more in the forests of Central and South America. It is believed to spend a great deal of its time in the trees.

Both Margays and Ocelots have been reared as pets and their handsome appearance has made them highly sought after but if you think of owning one remember that they may become unpredictable and even dangerous as they get older. Even more important is the danger to the species created by the demand for them. In obtaining one kitten to become a pet, trappers may have killed or mained many more. You may find a kitten bred in captivity but even keeping that may encourage irresponsible attitudes in others.

The Jaguarondi (*Felis jaguaroundi*) is nothing like a jaguar but the most weasel-like of cats. Up to $2\frac{1}{2}$ ft long, plus 18 in of tail, they range through similar territory to the ocelot and margay, living in savannahs and on forest fringes. Despite their short legs they climb and run easily living largely on birds, especially ground-dwelling ones, and eating fruit directly from the trees. They may have grey or reddish coats but both types are indistinctly blotched and striped.

The Tiger Cat (*Felis tigrina*) is like a slightly smaller version of the Margay and overlaps its territory from Costa Rica to northern South America. A good climber, it likes forest and woodland. This and the following three South American cats all have a greyish tinge to their fur.

The Mountain Cat (*Felis jacobita*) lives in the foothills of the Andes in Chile and is only about 18 in long plus a 9-in tail.

Geoffroy's Cat (*Felis geoffroyi*) lives in the uplands and foothills on the other side of the Andes from Bolivia to Patagonia. It climbs well and does not venture above the treeline.

The Pampas Cat (*Felis colocolo*) once lived in both the grasslands and swamps of Argentina and Uruguay but is now becoming increasingly rare. It is about the same size as a large domestic cat.

Pallas' Cat (*Felis manul*) is an unusual-looking and comparatively rare species found in Tibet, Mongolia and parts of Siberia. Its low-set ears and high set eyes may make it easier for it to hunt from the cover of rocky ledges. It is about the size of a domestic cat and has some long white body hairs with black tips which accentuate its silvery appearance.

That Flat-headed Cat (*Felis planiceps*), also has a strange appearance. One of the smallest cats, only 2 ft long including its tail, it lives on river banks in southern Asia, Borneo and Sumatra and eats fish and frogs but little is known about it.

The Bay Cat (*Felis badia*) is very rare and lives on the edge of the jungle. It is about the same size as the Flat-headed Cat but has a longer tail (about 6 in).

The Marbled Cat (*Felis marmorata*) is little bigger than a domestic cat but is more heavily furred and has a longer tail. It looks like a miniature Clouded Leopard and ranges from the Himalayas to Borneo and Sumatra where it lives along river banks and in jungle clearings. It has a reputation for being very fierce.

Temminck's Golden Cat (*Felis temmincki*) closely resembles the African Golden Cat although it is slightly larger with noticeable stripes on the head and neck. It ranges from Tibet through to Sumatra.

The Chinese Desert Cat (*Felis bieti*) which lives in the dry grasslands and in the semi-deserts on the edge of the west Chinese and Tibetan steppes is similar to, but smaller than, the African Wild Cat and lacks its bold markings. The light coat may serve to reflect the sun's heat as well as providing good camouflage. It has a slight ear tuft.

The Fishing Cat (*Felis viverrina*) is about $2\frac{1}{2}$ ft long plus a further 10 in of tail. It likes thick cover near waterways and has slightly webbed toes. It has not been scientifically observed to hunt in water but is said to eat fish and snails. It ranges from India and Indo-China to Java and Sumatra. The name is an exact translation of the Bengali "Mach-bagral".

The Rusty-spotted Cat (*Felis rubiginosa*) of South India and Sri-Lanka lives in long grass and brushwood and if captured when young is easily tamed. It is little over 2 ft from nose to tail tip.

The Leopard Cat (*Felis bengalensis*) is a little larger and ranges from south-east Asia to the Phillipines and northwards to Tibet and Siberia. It seems to be a good swimmer and one has been reported to have built a nest up in a tree to rear its kittens, although other zoologists claim it is entirely ground-living. It is the most common wild cat of south-east Asia and lives in hilly areas, avoids thick forest and is largely nocturnal. The coat varies in colour through its terrain and is more heavily spotted in mainland Asia. Although it is a very beautiful cat with large eyes, its spotting is not arranged in rosettes as on the real leopard.

The domestic cat
Which of the smaller members of the cat family was it that developed into the Domestic Cat (*Felis catus*)? The similarities between the modern wild cats and the house cat are so great and the differences — largely a matter of size, fur length and the hard protective pads of the wild cat's paws — so few that it is difficult to establish any authentic genealogy. It is quite likely that in different parts of the world different local species became the first domestic cats. The Rusty-spotted Cat of Southern India and Sri-Lanka may be the ancestor of the spotted cats of India, whilst the European Wild Cat looks like a very heavily built Tabby and can successfully interbreed with domestic cats.

One theory which receives wide support is that the Domestic Cat evolved from the cross breeding of *Felis sylvestris* and *Felis lybica* but zoologists far from agree on the matter. It is believed that cats were first domesticated in Egypt and the majority of a group of 192 cat mummies preserved in the British Museum are *Felis lybica*.

In nature, every species produces the occasional mutation or freak but they are isolated instances and rarely persist since evolutionary change takes many generations. When man is around to control mating the situation is very different and by carefully nurturing and perpetuating mutant variations he has created the wide variety of breeds which characterize many of the domestic animals we know today. Cats have lived more independent lives than other domestic species and do not display the enormous range of size, shape and colour that has been produced in, say, the dog. But varieties of domestic cats now exist which in shape, coat and colour would never have been spontaneously created in the wild. However uncertain we may be of the genealogy of *Felis catus* there is no doubt at all that the breeds represented in this book owe their existence in their present form entirely to the hand of man.

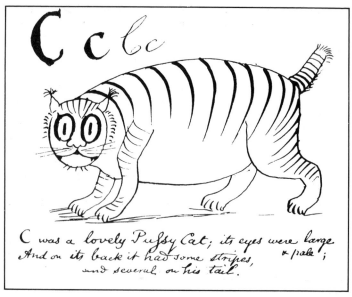

C was a lovely Pussy Cat; its eyes were large & pale; And on its back it had some stripes, and several on his tail.

A Cat *by Edward Lear, artist and nonsense writer who wrote* The Owl and the Pussy Cat *and invented the Runcible Cat*

CATS AND MAN

Most of the animals domesticated by man began their relationship with him as a food source or as hunting companions but the cat's association with man has depended more on the advantage to the cat than on its use to human beings. There are many stories to explain the origin or the domestication of the cat. One told by the Hopi Indians of Arizona relates how a young boy found a strange animal under a rock, captured it and took it home. His father recognized it as a cat which was known to eat rabbits and rodents. The boy shut the cat in a hole in the wall and went out to catch a rabbit. He brought food for the cat until it became tame and made itself at home and cats have lived in Hopi houses ever since, keeping them free of mice and rats. Much more typical of the cat's nature is a story from old India. The people of the Khasi Hills in Assam describe a time when the cat lived with the tiger, her brother. He grew sick and began to shiver and she knew that she must find fire to warm him. But only man had fire. When she reached his house to ask for some there was no one there. She went in to take some fire but before she reached it she saw some tasty fish and some delicious rice on the floor. Unable to resist such a feast she helped herself and was just about to curl up for an after-dinner nap in front of the fire when she remembered why she had come. She took a burning brand between her teeth and ran back to her brother but as soon as she had kindled a fire to warm him she announced that she had found a new way of life and was going to live with man where there was good food for the taking and it was always warm.

We know that the cat did not become domesticated until much later than the dog and food animals such as cattle but it is impossible to know exactly when the transition was first made. In Switzerland archaeologists have found cat bones associated with prehistoric man but since they were accompanied by the bones of other wild carnivores it is unlikely that they were domesticated. A cat found in the Indus Valley has been dated at about 2000 BC and may have been domesticated but it is difficult to distinguish a wild cat from a domestic cat by bones alone. Archaeologists used to believe that domestic animals were always different in size but this is now disputed and there is perennial argument over the criteria which distinguish a domestic animal.

The earliest known picture of a cat was painted in an Egyptian tomb about 2600 BC – none has been discovered among prehistoric cave paintings. This cat is wearing a wide collar but it could still be a wild cat for, although the cat was established as the object of a religious cult in Egypt well before 2000 BC, the first unchallenged records of domestic cats date from only 1800 BC.

The Egyptians did not believe that every cat was a god but that it was a form in which some of their deities might be personified. It was in the shape of a cat that the great sun god Ra overcame Apep, the serpent of darkness. Delicate papyrus drawings show him dealing the death blow with a sharp knife, a victory which had to be repeated every day for both the sun and darkness are immortal. The Egyptian word for cat was Mau, derived from the cat's voice.

Another snake-killing deity was the goddess Mafdet, presented in cat form in pyramid wall carvings of the Fifth and Sixth Dynasties dating from before 2280 BC as protector of the pharaoh. Cat and cat's head amulets survive which are of about this date. Was there a practical basis for believing in the protective power of the cat? Did real cats keep real snakes from the palace and the home?

Bast and Sekhmet were two great goddesses worshipped in the Temple of the Sun at Heliopolis. Both were originally presented as lion-headed but later Bast (or Pasht or Bastet as she is variously known) was depicted as a cat or with a cat's head. Each of the Egyptian deities had an associated cult animal which was kept in their sanctuary as a representation of the god in physical form. They were so venerated that throughout the province which each god protected all his or her animals came to be considered sacred. This sometimes led to inter-provincial strife but Bast came to be so important that all cats were revered throughout Egypt. To eat or kill them was a crime.

At Bubastis, Bast's chief cult centre in Lower Egypt, the temple cats lived in the courtyard. Looking after them was a special honour which was passed from father to son. They were carefully watched by the priests who waited to interpret any message from the goddess. A devotee wishing to seek the goddess's aid or make a vow would partly shave the head of his child and take the clipped hair to the temple where it was balanced against its weight in silver. That sum was then presented to the guardian of the sacred cats who cut up a suitable amount of fish which was fed to them.

The Greek historian Herodotus, who visited Bubastis in 450 BC, records a number of strange things about cats. The males, he says, spurned by the females after kittening, steal the kittens, carry them away and kill them. "The females, being deprived of their young, and longing to supply their place, seek the males once more" and the males regain their companionship. If a fire broke out, he reported, people made no attempt to quell it. They stood about watching while cats rushed past them into the flames.

The Egyptians were very fond of their household cats which are shown on laps and under chairs in a number of paintings. They also trained them to retrieve when they went wildfowling on the marshes of the delta. Plutarch describes how carefully the Egyptians bred their cats, ensuring that tom and queen were of compatible character. If a cat died all the members of the household shaved their eyebrows off in mourning. To deliberately kill a cat was punishable by death and even an accidental death demanded a heavy fine. In Ptolemaic times a member of the Roman embassy who accidentally killed a cat was saved from a lynching only by the intervention of the pharaoh himself. In 500 BC a Persian king besieging an Egyptian

A cat mummy

The Goddess Bast

An Egyptian bronze

A bronze coffin for a cat

city ordered his men to round up all the cats he could and advanced upon the town with each soldier carrying a cat before him. The Egyptians dared not strike a blow for fear of killing the sacred cats and were forced to surrender.

Both temple and domestic cats were given formal burial and were usually mummified. Elaborate coffins and mummy cases have survived and at Bubastis, where cats were frequently sent for interment from other parts of the country, archaeologists discovered some 300,000 embalmed cats laid in tiers in subterranean tombs. Few of them were preserved, instead the bodies were used as fertilizer.

The Egyptians tried to prevent their cats being exported but many must have been smuggled out, and when Rome began to adopt some of the Egyptian religions she also began to take up the cat both as a cult animal and as a household pet. They were recommended for protecting gardens from mice and moles and their usefulness was soon recognized throughout the empire.

The Greeks, on the other hand, are often said to have had no time for cats. Literary references are almost non-existent although one character in a play does ridicule the Egyptian regard for them. It has been suggested that some of the cats which appear in carvings and vase paintings are not cats but martens or civets, but a funeral stele from the Athens Keramicos shows that one family cat was loved enough to earn a place on his master's gravestone.

It is not only in Egypt and Romano-Egyptian religions that the cat has played a part. The Chinese had an agricultural god in cat form, the Peruvians a feline god of copulation, the Irish a god with a cat's head and cats are linked with two nordic goddesses. As late as the end of the 15th century Pope Innocent VIII ordered the Inquisition to seek out cat worshippers.

The Christian Church identified the old religions with the devil and cats, especially black cats, were often thought to be the form taken by Satan himself. Medieval French peasants believed that the cat slept all day in order to keep watch in the barns and stables all night and warn the evil spirits of human approach so that they might disappear. In the 12th and 13th centuries the followers of the Waldensian and Albigensian heresies were accused of carrying out rites involving cats, and when Pope Clement V suppressed the order of Knights Templar early in the 14th century some of its members confessed under torture that they had worshipped the devil in the shape of a black tomcat. In this form the devil was also believed to have been responsible for an outbreak of St Vitus dance in Metz in 1344 and each year for more than four centuries thereafter the people of this French town publicly burned 13 cats in an iron cage. Similar ceremonies are reported from other European towns — perhaps the survival of a pagan rite which the Church had taken over, reversing its symbolism. At the coronation of Elizabeth I of England live cats were caged inside an effigy of the Pope to represent the devils which the protestants believed to control him. After being carried in procession the effigy and cats were burned upon a pyre.

The Christian persecution of the cat allowed the European rat population to grow unchecked and contributed to the virulence of rat-spread plagues.

The Church considered that all witches were in league with the devil but, while people on the Continent believed that a witch had the power to turn herself into an animal, the English believed that each had a "familiar", a lesser devil servant, who took animal form. It might be a toad, a dog, a rabbit – any creature – but a pet cat, especially a black cat, was responsible for many a lonely old woman being accused of witchcraft.

In the 17th century there was a surge of interest in witchcraft and witch-hunting, especially in England. King James I wrote a book about witches and a government Witchfinder was appointed. There were numerous confessions of strange intimacies with cats and of spell-making with their aid but they were sometimes extracted under torture or threat of torture and from women who were often psychologically disturbed. The persecution mania crossed the Atlantic to the American colonies where the notorious Salem witch trials took place in Massachusetts in 1692. One witness declared that he had been attacked by a she-devil which "came in at the Window in the likeness of a Cat. . .fell upon him, took fast hold of his Throat, lay on him a considerable while, and almost killed him." When he called on the Trinity it "leaped on the Floor and flew out at the Window."

When cats were not being treated as devils and savagely persecuted they were often – and are still today – considered to be symbols of good luck. Japanese sailors, for instance, always welcome a tortoiseshell cat as it is reputed to banish storm devils. In many parts of the world white cats are considered particularly lucky – although in Britain contrariwise it is the black cat which is supposed to bring luck. One rather macabre use of cat

Witches and their familiars. A woodcut from a broadsheet of 1619. "The Wonderful Discoverie of the Witchcrafts of Margaret and Phillip Flower"

magic which seems to have persisted until the early years of this century was to bury a cat in the walls or foundations of a building. This was sometimes interpreted as a means of keeping the place free of mice and rats but probably had its origin in a much older form of propitiatory building sacrifice of the kind which is still remembered in the coins and other objects which are often placed under foundation stones today.

In the south of France, in particular, there used to be a widespread belief in magician cats known as *matagots* who could bring prosperity to a house where they were loved and looked after. The world's folklore and fairytales include stories of a number of clever and helpful *matagots* such as Dick Whittington's cat, who brought fame and fortune to a Lord Mayor of London, and Puss in Boots whose cunning brought his master a king's daughter and a kingdom.

In the 16th century, Sir Henry Wyat, a prisoner in the Tower of London, did have his life improved by a cat which strayed into his dungeon. She helped to keep him warm and brought him pigeons that she caught. The keeper of the Tower was under orders to offer him the poorest food but the regulations did not prevent him from cooking food which the prisoner provided so Sir Henry was able to eat the birds which the cat had brought.

Another prisoner in the Tower, the young Earl of Southampton who was Shakespeare's patron, was painted with his favourite cat which, it is said, sought out her master and climbed down a chimney to join him during his imprisonment.

Through the centuries cats have been loved by nobles and commoners, rich and poor alike, and there are countless stories of their exploits, both real and in literature. Mohammed is said to have loved cats, and to have given the tabby its forehead making of an "M" (though since this is not an arabic letter it sounds like an invented legend!). The Hindus use a word for cat which means "the cleanest". Only Christians seem to have persecuted cats; but although the Church feared the cat for its links with the old beliefs it was not only in the East that its value was appreciated. The cat's practical virtues have never been more clearly recognized than in the ancient Welsh laws which enumerate its worth at different ages according to its physical perfection and mousing abilities: one assessment made a cat worth a whole barn of wheat.

Through the ages, writers, painters and musicians have used their talents to venerate their pets. A Medieval monk penned this poem to his feline companion:

> When a mouse darts from its den,
> O how glad is Pangur then!
> O what gladness do I prove
> When I solve the doubts I love!
>
> So in peace our tasks we ply,
> Pangur Ban, my cat, and I:
> In our arts we find our bliss,
> I have mine and he has his.

A vampire cat of Japanese legend. One tale tells of a cat which killed the Prince of Hizen's "favourite lady", took her form and then, while he slept, drained him of his blood. In Japanese folklore all cats are clever but the wicked ones are easily identified by their double tails

T. S. Eliot's *Old Possum's Book of Cats* portrays no less than 14 individualistic felines, together with a poem *The Naming of Cats*. Christopher Smart's strange and wonderful verses, written in an 18th-century madhouse, about his cat Jeoffrey who . . . "purrs in thankfulness, when God tells him he's a good Cat" . . . are a favourite with all cat lovers; they have been included in Benjamin Britten's setting of parts of the complete poem, *Jubilate Agno*. Ravel included two very different cats, a comic pair of Siamese, in his *L'Enfant et les sortilèges* set to a libretto by Colette, herself a great felinophile whose cat regularly sat upon her desk while she wrote.

John Rich, the 18th-century actor-manager who first presented *The Beggar's Opera* demonstrated his affection for the species by keeping no less than 27 cats. But probably no single cat was ever so indulged as Samuel Johnson's Hodge for whom the learned Doctor himself went out to buy oysters.

Famous cats and famous cat owners are legion but let the words of the 16th-century French essayist Montaigne stand for the relationship which all cat owners will recognize when he writes about his cat:

"When my cat and I entertain each other with mutual apish tricks, as playing with a garter, who knows but I make my cat more sport than she makes me? Shall I conclude her simple, that has her time to begine or refuse to play as freely as I myself have? Nay, who knows but that it is a defect of my not understanding her language (for doubtless cats talk and reason with one another) that we agree no better? And who knows but that she pities me for being no wiser than to play with her, and laughs and censures my folly for making sport with her, when we two play together?"

Detail of the title page of Des Chats, *a book of pictures by Theophile Steinlen, an artist famous for his cat pictures. Through the centuries many artists have delighted in depicting the cat from Breughel and Leonardo da Vinci to Foujita and Ronald Searle*

THE DOMESTIC CAT

If you are to keep your cat happy and healthy it is important that you think of it as a cat, an animal with natural instincts and character, and do not endow it with human ideas and reactions. Any animal reared by humans in a domestic environment will to some extent become imprinted towards them and adopt habits which would be alien to it in the wild, but cats which go feral and readily survive on their own are an indication of how light their veneer of domestication is. Their natural cunning and resourcefulness enable them to take advantage of domestic opportunities but the pattern of their behaviour is little changed from that of their wild relations. Sociologists and anthropologists have shown how close to the surface the primitive instincts and behaviour forms are in ourselves so it is not surprising that this should clearly be true of the cat.

The cat is a carnivore and a predator and its body is a very efficient machine developed to surprise, capture, consume and digest the animals on which it lives. It is not designed for prolonged bouts of activity and a cat will tire more rapidly than a human but, for its size, it is tremendously strong — as you will know if you have ever tried to hold a cat that is determined to struggle free or seen a cat smack really hard with one of its forepaws.

A cat's spine, though very like our own, allows it to bend and arch its back in a much more pliable way than man's skeleton permits; it can turn its

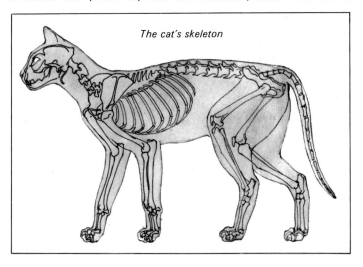

The cat's skeleton

head almost through 180°, and its forelegs can be moved without undue strain in almost any direction, making the whole body extremely flexible. This versatile frame is operated by powerful muscles which are especially strong in the back legs, giving a powerful spring, and in the neck and shoulders. The muscles can take considerable strain but the heart and lungs cannot, which is why cats cannot sustain a high level of activity for very long. Konrad Lorenz has pointed out that a half-hour leisurely stroll with a human will tire even a strong and healthy adult cat. The chest cavity of the cat is relatively small for its size and consequently its heart and lungs are too. Compare the breathing of a relaxed or sleeping cat with your own: you will find that even when making no effort of any kind the cat still breathes more than twice as many times a minute as you do yourself. Its heart rate will range from about 110 to 240 beats per minute, and in kittens will race as fast as 300 beats per minute. While these hard-working organs are comparatively small, the cat's digestive system takes up a proportionately large amount of space. In the wild a cat may go for considerable periods between meals and so there has to be space for it to eat large quantities when it has killed its prey and to absorb it slowly during a period which may be without hunting success.

The part of the brain that controls the cat's mobility is particularly well developed to give lightning reactions in all areas of muscular movement, balance and directional control, but a responsive and well-tuned body is not enough to make a successful predator. The sensory system feeding information to the brain must be efficient and highly developed to enable it to catch its prey and elude enemies. Except for taste, which is of minor importance in the battle for survival, the cat's senses have great range and sensitivity.

Sight

In most mammals smell plays the major role in recognition, in guiding them to food and in warning them of danger but the cat, along with man and the monkeys, relies primarily upon the evidence of its eyes. All cats' eyes are large in comparison with the size of their skull and their sight is extremely sensitive. They are placed well forward so that both eyes cover the same field of view to give stereoscopic vision (unlike animals with eyes on the side of their heads which register two quite separate images). This helps to make cats remarkable judges of distance and it is extremely rare for one to miscalculate a jump. Each eye can see through an angle of nearly 205° and coupled with the flexibility of the neck, which enables them to scan a wide field with minimum movement, this gives them very wide coverage. A cat's eyes do not have as sensitive a response to colour as our own. Until recently it was thought that they saw only in monochrome but it is now estimated that they average one cone (which registers colour) on the retina to over twenty to twentyfive rods (which register light intensity). Humans have one to four. Cats also seem less able to see stationary objects sharply or to focus at very close quarters. If they do not see a plaything land, and it does so without a noise, cats often have great difficulty in finding it and they seem to rely upon smell to locate food that is, literally, right under their nose. In bright light they may also be at a disadvantage but the iris of the eye can close up to leave only a narrow slit and reduce the amount of light passing through the lens.

In dim light cats are at a tremendous advantage. The iris opens until the pupil becomes a full circle allowing the maximum possible light to enter the eye; then the light strikes a triangular area in the upper part of the eye, known as the *tapetum lucidum*, where the retinal cells are backed by large flat cells which act as a mirror reflecting the light that has not been absorbed in passing through the eye back to the retinal cells. When you see a cat's eyes apparently shining in the dark it is the *tapetum lucidum* which is reflecting back the available light. This means of intensifying light, which the cat shares with other nocturnal animals, enables it to see in conditions which we would consider pitch darkness.

The cat also has an extra eyelid, known as the nictitating membrane or less technically as the haw, which closes upwards from the inner corner of the eye. This is not opaque and allows some vision when drawn across the eye. It reduces the intensity of very bright light, affords some protection from eye damage in a fight or in pushing through prickly undergrowth and it helps to clean the eye. When a cat is ill the haw will often stay partially closed but this can occasionally occur with cats that are perfectly healthy.

Touch

When it becomes so dark that even the cat cannot see it must rely upon its other senses. The cat can feel its way about to a degree that only the blind, perhaps, can fully comprehend. It is not simply that the

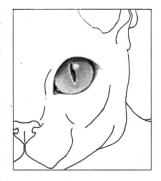

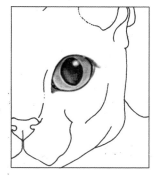

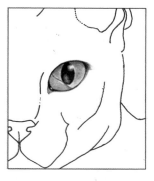

The cat's eyes:
iris closed
iris open
nictitating membrane

29

cat has a highly developed sense of touch — its skin is covered with highly sensitive "touch spots:" which respond to the lightest pressure — its whiskers and eyebrows and the group of long hairs on the back of its forepaws all transmit pressure sensations to the brain. Most of us have felt the sensation in the dark of something which we cannot see being in the way, an awareness caused by the changes in air pressure due to the presence of an obstruction. Cats have this ability to an enhanced degree, particularly through these long hairs and whiskers, known as vibrissae, which are sensitive to minute variations in air pressure. It is an old fallacy that the width of a cat's whiskers matches the size of its body and enables it to judge whether it can get through a space but they do play a major role in spatial orientation and, in the dark, dewhiskered cats will bump into things.

In daylight a cat will often use touch to investigate an object. The front paws are particularly sensitive and there is a large part of its brain devoted to their touch perception. The nose is also highly touch-sensitive and will frequently be used in conjunction with the paws. The lightest touch on a cat's back will send a shiver down its spine if it is unexpected, but touch also gives them considerable pleasure — is there a cat alive that does not enjoy being stroked? Perhaps it creates a sense of well being and security by its similarity to the washing movements of its mother's tongue.

Hearing
The cat's hearing can detect sounds over a very wide range — from 30 to 45,000 cycles per second. Except for the very lowest notes, we can hear about as well as the cat up to around 2,000 cycles but from then until 4,000 cycles — the range when human hearing is at its best — the cat excels us and its optimum range continues up to about 8,000 cycles. Most humans reach the limit of their range with the topmost notes on a violin — about 20,000 cycles — but the cat's hearing does not begin noticeably to fade until 40,000 cycles and some cats do not appear to reach their limit until around 60,000 cycles! To complement this enormous range the cat's ears are shaped and ridged to concentrate the sound and they are highly manoeuvrable so that having detected the slightest noise they can focus their hearing upon its source. When you hear a noise from outside a room you register it along with all the other noises but a cat will immediately concentrate on the point from which the sound entered the room: the section of window that is open, a ventilation grill or a crack beneath the door. A cat will often locate an object hidden from vision by the sound of its fall. It will distinguish and differentiate sounds at a much greater distance than we can: hearing your footsteps as you turn the corner of the street and recognizing your car's engine from all others even when it seems to be asleep.

Balance
The inner ear of the cat appears to be formed like our own but there must be some vital difference since most dogs and many humans suffer from travel sickness at some time during their life while cats appear to be immune

to the effects of a boat's rocking or a car's movement. This immunity is obviously related to their phenomenal sense of balance which enables them to right themselves when falling and to make a safe landing. A cat born deaf — and this seems to be a congenital defect in pure white cats with blue eyes — will retain this sense of equilibrium. Even a cat lacking the entire inner ear was able to right itself — but it did not attempt to do so when it had been blindfolded. This righting ability clearly involves other senses and does not appear to operate if both sight and hearing are lacking. Although cats have fallen from considerable heights without injury they could be in great danger if, when half asleep, they should slip, from a window ledge for instance, as their senses may not be aroused until too late to save them from serious injury. And, although they can make a perfect four-point landing from a great height, the impact of landing may cause injury to their legs or jaw. Falls from very short distances, such as from a child's arms, can also be damaging because the drop is not long enough to give them time to turn the body into the landing position.

Vocalization

The cat has a considerable vocal range, from the chirruping noises used when a mother talks to her kittens to the full-throated call of a Siamese on heat. Marvin Clark, a blind musician whose hearing was ultra-sensitive, believed that he could distinguish 100 different sounds in the cat's vocabulary. Most cat owners are unlikely to identify even a quarter of that number of different "words" but there are many easily recognizable sounds which become established in human-feline conversation, including the familiar miaow which is used when "talking" to humans but rarely to another cat. Various requests and demands, greetings and

The cat can right itself while falling and make a remarkable landing on all four feet

expressions of satisfaction – even perhaps a handful of swear words – soon become familiar, but a wider understanding demands close observation and affinity. Physical expressions, particularly positions of the tail and the ears will also convey a great deal of information, particularly about a cat's emotional state. An erect tail and ears show that a cat is happy and interested. A waving tail is also a sign of pleasure but if it lashes from side to side this demonstrates annoyance and a twitching tip to the tail shows contained irritation.

The purr of cats is a sign of pleasure, although a deeper and harsher purr may be made by cats in pain or when they are particularly apprehensive – perhaps in a determination to suppress the agony by a process of self-delusion. Adult cats often purr on several notes but sometimes the purr is silent to human ears although its vibrations can be felt. The mechanism of purring is only beginning to be understood. Investigations by a French veterinarian show that it is produced by the vocal cords and that the muscles of the larynx contract rythmically to produce the throbbing sound. It is possible that the resonance is produced from the diaphragm.

Taste
Taste does not play an important part in feline life, but any cat owner will have noticed their pet's preference for certain flavours thereby disproving the once-held theory that cats had no sense of taste. Most of the cat's taste buds are on the tongue with a few on the soft palate and the surrounding parts of the mouth. Adults are most sensitive to sour tastes and sweetness produces the least sensation.

Smell
Although sight is most important to them when hunting, the sense of smell is strongly developed in cats and appears to give them a tremendous amount of pleasure. It is a major means of identification at both long and short range. The fact that a cat can fail to see food that is directly before it and relies upon its nose for locating it exactly is probably the result of the first few days of life when, before its eyes are open, the kitten relies upon its sense of smell to find its mother's nipple.

Watch a cat sitting by an open window and sniffing in the hundreds of fascinating scents upon the breeze, some of the most interesting probably being the very smells which humans find so unpleasant! To intensify a particular odour the cat will open its mouth and gasp in more air. A cat will also enjoy investigating the scent records of its owner's travels, or those of another animal, sniffing out all the traces left upon your hands or clothing which tell of where you have been and whom you met.

Smell plays a vital role in territory marking and in sexual identification. Even if a female cat does not make loud mating calls, her scent will advertise for a considerable distance that she is on heat. When a cat rubs itself against a person or a piece of furniture it may also be leaving a scent marking (although not in the pungent way of male territory identification), especially when it rubs its head against the hand in a very typical feline gesture, for there are scent glands on the side of a cat's head.

Territory

As predatory carnivores, the members of the cat family mark out a range of territory which they are rarely prepared to share with others of the same species. Since moving in with man, and particularly in an urban situation, the domestic cat has been forced to accept a shared terrain and is able to do so because he relies more upon humans than on hunting for his food supply. However, many cats will still chase intruders out of a limited area – their own garden, for instance – and will often try to avoid using common thoroughfares at the same time as other neighbourhood cats. Known neighbours will be tolerated in a way that strangers would not be and territories may cross, but even feline friends will be kept off a favourite spot and within the house a particular place may be claimed and defended against all comers.

The unneutered male will mark his territory by spraying urine, impregnating the boundaries and landmarks of his demesne with his own odour – a smell which is extremely difficult to expunge or even disguise. For many owners this is reason enough for having a male kitten castrated. The simple operation also removes the urge to go on long midnight prowls in search of females and reduces the likelihood of becoming involved in fights. More importantly it means one less male to father unwanted kittens.

Hunting

Although house pets no longer have to catch and kill their own food, the cat's body and instincts are designed and developed to make it a very skilful hunter and a few thousand years of domestication have not blunted its abilities. Watch any litter of kittens at play and you will see that almost

An Abyssinian "freezes" while out hunting

all of the games are actually exercises in hunting skills. They are trying out the techniques which you can observe in the adult cat stalking its prey. The way in which a kitten approaches a ball is a rehearsal for catching a mouse and the attack on a dangling plaything uses identical movements to those with which it would try to catch a bird.

The experienced cat may wait patiently along a track it knows its prey may use, staying motionless for hours yet always ready for a sudden spring, or it may stealthily stalk its prey. Cats love high places from which they can survey the terrain, spotting quarry, danger or just interesting incidents. They will equally conceal themselves to spy out the lie of the land from secure cover. Even indoors you will find them on the top step of a decorator's ladder the moment your back is turned or insinuating themselves beneath a sheet of newspaper that has fallen on the floor.

When scent, sound or movement inform a cat of the presence of prey (or convey any intriguing or disturbing message) he will concentrate all his senses for a moment to obtain the greatest possible information. He may emerge from cover to investigate the situation further, often taking a circuitous route to avoid being observed. Unless he knows himself to be in reliable cover, a cat moves in short sharp bursts, keeping his body as close to the ground as possible. The nearer he gets to his quarry the more carefully he approaches, stopping frequently to assess the situation, lowering his ears to reduce his visible area and listening carefully before advancing further. There will be a trembling moment of preparation, then a sudden dash from cover or a lightning pounce with outstretched paws and his teeth and claws are grasping the creature or the toy.

An insect will be snatched at by the jaws but other prey will usually be killed by a neat and decisive bite on the neck and, like most small carnivores, the cat will eat from the head (or sometimes with birds from the wing-base) downwards.

In natural conditions, mother cats will often bring still-living prey to their kittens and train them in catching and killing, but a cat which has never killed to eat may never associate killing with food and if a kitten does not make a kill at a particular responsive period in its adolescence it may never learn to do so. Although the method of biting the neck appears to be an inherited response set off by chasing the prey, it is not instinctive but has to be learned.

Attack and defence
Kittens at play will rarely hurt each other, no matter how ferocious their games appear to be, for a restraining instinct sheaths their claws. Although litter mates may trigger off the instincts to chase or pounce, the initial victim of an ambush may quickly switch to playing the predator.

Even as adults, cats do not often take on a real fight, despite the evidence to the contrary of torn-eared toms. Cats will almost always give plenty of warning before launching an attack and will first try to engage in a psychological confrontation consisting of a display of strength and an exchange of threatening and submissive signals until one of the contenders gives way.

Two cats will stand glaring at each other for minutes at a time before either makes a further move. The bristling fur and fluffed out tail which make a cat look bigger and perhaps more formidable are a reaction of fear and will remain for some time after a cat has made its escape. In fact, the familiar arched-back posture is a mixture of defensive and aggressive signals. Dilated eyes, open mouth and laid-back ears are all considered by zoologists to be defensive postures, while stiff legs and raised tail are symbols of attack. The rear quarters advance to attack whilst the foreparts retreat, or at most stand their ground, forcing the back to arch.

Hissing and spitting is a warning signal and the loud explosive noise that a cat can make may sufficiently shock an aggressive dog, for instance, to enable the cat to escape before the dog can recover. A sudden attack may also be used to disengage a larger enemy's concentration — this is not so much an attempt to inflict serious damage but rather to provide an opportunity for escape during the ensuing confusion. Unless it is really cornered a cat will rarely try to tackle an aggressor but will rapidly put a safe distance between the threat and itself. It is unlikely that you will ever see a cat go to join a fight, unless it is sure it is only a playful one.

If a real fight cannot be avoided a cat will attack with the claws of the forepaws, which are very sharp and can inflict a deep gash, and with its teeth if it is possible to get close enough to the enemy without getting its own face scratched. Bite wounds are rare in cat fights unless the opponents are ill-matched. A losing cat will usually adopt a defensive position by throwing itself on its back so that it can strike out at its opponent with all

A real fight cannot always be avoided

four sets of claws; it will concentrate in particular on delivering savage blows with its powerful hind legs.

The same fighting techniques will be used in confrontations with humans. First a verbal complaint if you are doing something it does not like, then a token scratch, then a real scratch or bite to give a chance for escape while you recover. If the situation really looks dangerous for a cat it will rapidly make itself scarce, or reach a safe vantage point from which it can scream abuse at you.

It is not a good idea to play fighting games with your cat with your bare hands – in its excitement it may misjudge and wound you – but generally cats are extremely careful not to hurt their friends. Claws that are out one moment as it runs up your coat will be sheathed the next to nestle on the thin fabric of a shirt or blouse. The soft pads of the paws make a cat's movements very quiet – a great asset for a hunter – but not so quiet that other cats cannot hear them. The claws of oriental cats are not so retractile as other breeds and make a clear click-clack noise as they approach across a hard surface.

A taste for order

Cats are fastidious creatures. They like to keep themselves and their surroundings clean. Faeces are meticulously buried and the coat is kept scrupulously clean. In fact, grooming takes up a great deal of a cat's time. It can reach most of its body with its tongue which acts as both sponge and comb, and its head and the back of its neck are kept clean by wetting the forepaws and using them as a scrubbing brush. They do not like loud noises or sudden movements and will usually take cover if they are present during a domestic row even when it has nothing to do with them. They are creatures of habit and like to have their regular times for each activity – especially meals and being let in and out – and regular places for sleeping, eating or watching the world. They will not be pleased if the furniture is rearranged or their regular routes are blocked – although they will study all developments with wary interest. There is not much a cat will miss. Cats are not without a sense of humour and will share and even play a joke but they will not relish being the butt of one.

THE CAT IN THE HOME

Looking after a cat does not require special skills, only commonsense, consideration and an awareness of responsibility. But before deciding to keep a cat remember that you will have to find time to feed and groom it, change litter or let it in and out, arrange for it to be cared for if you are away and meet the cost of food, litter and veterinary bills.

There are many lovely breeds to choose from, or you may lose your heart to a kitten of obscure origin. Character belongs more to the individual than the breed, although some have greater need of human company. If a cat is to be kept indoors then think of having two for one may be very lonely on its own.

No reputable breeder or pet dealer will knowingly offer an unhealthy cat for sale but you should nevertheless be on the look out for danger signs whether you are buying a pedigree kitten or an ordinary moggy. If you adopt a stray or take on a kitten from a neighbour's litter take the same precautions. Infections and ailments cannot always be prevented in the best of homes and speedy treatment will prevent worse problems later. Look out for black specks or small hard granules like sawdust on the coat, they may be flea droppings or lice. Check the ears to make sure the insides are clean and free of mites — a cat that is continually shaking its head or scratching its ears may have an infestation. Are the eyes clear and bright? If the inner eyelid (haw) is partially closed it may be a sign of sickness. Look out for coughs and sneezes. Is the stomach distended — a sign of gastric problems — or are there any signs of diarrhoea? Are the legs strong with no trace of lameness? Is the kitten lively and playful? Take a look inside the kitten's mouth, it should be a rosy pink, and make sure it has all its teeth for if it has not it is too young to be sold. Kittens less than six weeks old should not be sold and they should preferably reach eight weeks or more before they go to a new home.

The breeder may give you a diet sheet and you should certainly find out what food the kitten has been having. If it is a pedigree cat you should receive a copy of the pedigree certificate (see page 76). Always ask whether a kitten has been vaccinated against Panleukopaenia (Feline Infectious Enteritis). If it has make sure you are given the vaccination certificate for you will need to know what kind of vaccine was used and when the booster injections will be required. Panleukopaenia is one of the most dangerous of feline diseases and if a kitten has not already been vaccinated you should arrange for it to be done as soon as possible.

Neutering

A check up at the vet's is a sensible precaution with any new kitten and at the same time you can make arrangements for the cat to be neutered if you do not intend to keep it for breeding purposes. Males can be neutered at any age from about 12 weeks old but the younger the cat the simpler the operation. A general anaesthetic will be given so you will be asked not to feed the cat for at least 12 hours before the operation. Although the actual castration takes only a few moments you will be asked to leave the cat at the surgery for several hours to make sure that it has fully recovered from the anaesthetic. Spaying — the removal of the uterus and ovaries of the female — requires more complicated surgery but is still a routine operation which vets perform dozens of times every week. Some vets prefer to carry it out when the cat is only about 10 weeks old and not yet fully developed, others prefer to wait until it is adult. A small patch of fur will be shaved off to facilitate the operation and the incision will have to be stitched, so the female should be restrained from being too active for the following few days to avoid putting strain upon the wound. You will have to make a second visit to the surgery to have the stitches taken out.

You may wish to delay spaying a cat until it has had a litter but unless you intend to become a serious breeder you would be misguided to keep whole cats for the world is already too full of unwanted kittens. With a female you can yourself accept the responsibility for providing or finding a good home for all her litter but with an unneutered tom you have no means of knowing how many kittens he may be fathering. If you have a whole tomcat he will spray urine to mark his territory and you will find this an extremely pungent and unpleasant smell to have on your walls and furniture. Have toms neutered young for if castrated after adulthood they have been known to continue in the habit.

The new kitten

Arrange to collect a new kitten only when you have plenty of time to help it settle into its new home, and when there will not be a lot of people or noise to frighten it. A stout well-fastened basket or a cardboard box of a kind approved by animal welfare organizations will be best to take it home. You will already have made friends with the kitten and on the journey home give it some attention — but do not let it out of the basket. If you have a very long journey it may be better to encourage the kitten to sleep by using a box which is kept closed except for ventilation holes.

If you have other pets try to keep them out of the way at first so that the kitten can adjust to its strange surroundings before having to face strange animals as well. When you do introduce them do not leave them alone together until you are quite sure that they have accepted each other. This is as much for the established animal's sake for the new arrival may panic and lash out with its claws. Give the established pet plenty of attention so that it does not become jealous.

Let the kitten explore its new home and gain confidence in it. Don't just let it run wild but try a room at a time and keep a careful watch to make sure that it comes to no harm. Talk to it gently, pet it often and make it feel really wanted. Show it its sanitary tray (it may need it badly) and offer a saucer of slightly warmed milk on arrival but do not try to feed it until it has settled down. When it begins to give itself a thorough wash you will know it has decided that its new surroundings are not so bad after all — and then is the time to produce some food to reassure it further. An older cat will probably take longer to get used to a new home.

Feeding
To begin with try to give the kitten the food to which it is already accustomed. Then, when it has settled it, you can gradually introduce changes in its diet if you wish. At eight weeks a kitten should be fully weaned and eating four varied meals a day. It must have meat — an all fish diet may lead to skin disease — and most kittens will enjoy a little breakfast cereal mixed in with their food, or some rice pudding mixed with a little evaporated milk. A saucer of cow's milk may be acceptable but beware, it can cause diarrhoea and some cats, especially some orientals, never acquire a taste for it. *Always* have fresh water available. Canned, dried and sachet-packed proprietary foods can be introduced as the cat gets older but many people prefer not to offer them to kittens. If you do feed them, even to adult cats, do not let them form the entire diet, however varied the descriptions on the labels seem to be. If a cat does not seem to drink much avoid the dried foods or urinary problems may develop.

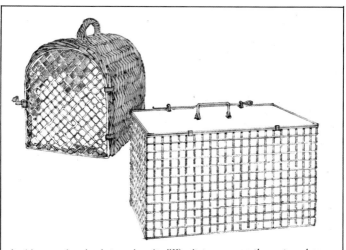

A side-opening basket makes it difficult to remove the cat and some cats can tear a hole in wickerwork. Plastic-covered metal mesh is strong and easily disinfected — but line the sides with paper on cold days

Up to the age of three months the kitten's stomach is no bigger than a walnut so meals must be small and frequent. A breakfast of milk and cereal, lunch of diced raw beef, scrambled egg and milk for tea and a meat supper, occasionally varied by offering *cooked* and boned white fish instead of meat, would be a good regimen at this age. Always feed a cat in the same place — somewhere you will not trip over it or its bowls, nor spill a saucepan or splash water — and use a food bowl that cannot be easily tipped over if the cat puts its paw on the edge. Cats often like to pull food out of the bowl on to the floor so you will be well advised to lay a newspaper as a tablecloth or place food dishes on an easily cleaned tray. And remember to have a bowl of fresh water constantly available.

At four months the kitten may begin to lose its milk teeth — you may not even notice it happening — and by six months it should have its adult set and be down to only two meals a day. Eventually you can make it just one big meal (serving about half an ounce per pound body weight for an adult cat) but you may prefer to keep to both morning and evening meals.

By all means indulge your cat's fads and fancies, provided that you still provide a balanced diet of carbohydrates, protein, minerals and vitamins, but if you don't want to be bullied into serving smoked salmon and double cream you may have to be tough. It will not harm an adult cat to go without a meal. If it will not eat what you give it do not leave the food to go bad. Take it away but offer nothing else. When the cat gets really hungry it will soon come round to eating what you give it. However, watch for the cat that is genuinely off its food for this is usually a sign of something wrong.

Some cats will enjoy gnawing on a large bone but remember that cooking makes bones brittle so never serve cooked fish or meat still on the bone and always remove all small bones which could get stuck in the cat's mouth or throat. In the wild, cats eat the stomach contents of their prey and thus obtain some vegetable food. The house cat should therefore be offered vegetables occasionally cooked because they do not find them easy to digest — and if they do not have access to outdoor grass some should be grown indoors for them to nibble from time to time. The cat uses grass as roughage and sometimes an an emetic to help it bring up balls of fur which accumulate from the hair it swallows when washing itself. They particularly like Cocksfoot Grass (*Dactylis glomerata*) and a pot will perhaps save the cat from nibbling at your other house plants which may make it sick. Do not grow philodendrons or dieffenbachia as house plants — both are poisonous to cats. Philodendrons produce a slow poison, dieffenbachias a rapid one. Laurel is also poisonous.

Bedding
There are a variety of cat beds and baskets available through pet stores. The traditional ones are made of wicker and the most modern are probably made of plastic or fibreglass. The latter will be the easiest to clean and disinfect. A new kitten will want a place to call its own and until it decides to choose somewhere else you should provide a bed; but there is no need to buy a special basket — a cardboard box makes an effective bed and can

be replaced when it gets dirty. When it first arrives a hot-water bottle under the blanket will replace the warmth a kitten has been used to getting from his mother and litter mates and a loudly-ticking clock (an alarm clock is ideal – but make sure the alarm is off) tucked alongside will give a reassuring beat like its mother's heart. Do not leave the bottle in the bed when it has gone cold or it will have the opposite effect.

In practice many cats will not want a basket at all. They will chose their own favourite place to sleep. However, if you do not want it to curl up on the foot of your bed or in the corner of an armchair you should make up a box or basket with several layers of newspaper as bedding, topped with a sheet or blanket which can be easily washed and put them in a warm, draught-free corner. Get down on the floor and see for yourself if you can feel a draught. You will not be able to tell while standing up! If you raise the bed an inch or two off the floor it may help.

Scratching post

If you want to protect your furniture and carpets from your cat's claws you should buy or make a scratching post – or train the cat to scratch only on one piece you are prepared to sacrifice. Pet shops often stock scratching pads impregnated with catnip but a piece of old carpet or coarse sacking glued to a wooden post, or to a thick cardboard roll of the kind from which cloth is sold, do better for some cats. A non-splintery log is another excellent alternative. Try to choose a texture for the scratching surface that is not matched elsewhere in the house and it will be easier to restrict the cat to this one place.

A scratching post and litter tray – vital equipment for indoor cats

Cats are not sharpening their claws, as many people think, when they scratch. They are stretching and exercising their claws and removing the worn outer covering of the front claws to reveal the sharp new point beneath. The cat uses its teeth to remove the worn outer layer from the back claws.

Litter tray

A vital piece of equipment, even if you eventually intend to let your cat out of doors, is a shallow tray which can be filled with sand, ash, sawdust or proprietary litter. You will find an enamel or plastic tray, which can be easily cleaned and disinfected, measuring about 18 in by 12 in with sides about 3 in high, will prove best, and can be obtained cheaply from pet stores. Although the specially formulated litter will be more expensive its moisture- and odour-absorbing properties make it worth trying. To make it go further lay a wad of newspaper in the bottom of the tray and scatter only a handful of litter on top. If you change the tray every day your cat may find this acceptable. Peat is used by many people but it can retain germs and must be rotted in the garden compost heap so that the high temperatures developed will kill them off.

Other equipment

You will also need a brush for grooming and an open-toothed comb, too, for long-haired cats. If your cat is not able to go outdoors its claws may

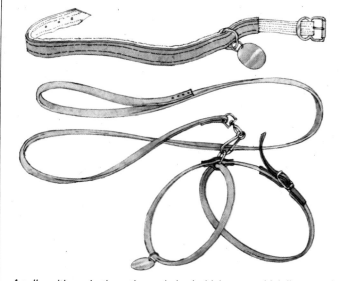

A collar with an elastic section and a lead with harness which fits around chest and body

42

grow more rapidly than they wear down and need trimming occasionally. This should be done with strong nail clippers — your vet will show you how. If yours is to be an outdoor cat you will want a collar and an identity disc engraved with its name and your address. Make sure that the collar has an elasticated section so that if it should get caught on a twig or a nail the cat can wriggle out of it and not be trapped. If you hope to teach your cat to walk out with you you will need a leash and may prefer a harness to a collar as it will put less strain upon the cat. If you live a long way from a chemist or a veterinarian you may want to keep a first-aid box of medicaments suitable for your cat, though your own treatments will usually serve if used correctly — usually in a diluted form. But be warned. *Never* adminster *aspirin* to cats; *never* disinfect them or anything to do with them with *carbolic; never* dust them with *DDT*.

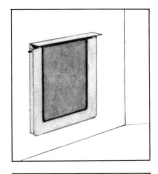

You may also like to buy or make your cat some toys. Pet shops often have fabric mice stuffed with catnip, the smell of which most cats like (some orientals excepted) and with which they enjoy playing. A table tennis ball, a piece of string, a cotton reel, a sheet of newspaper and a crumpled ball of paper will also give them endless pleasure. The games they can play with them are only limited by the range of your own and your cat's invention. You may soon find you have a budding football star or a prize retriever.

A cat-door set into the wall or the panel of a door will give your cat access to the house without having to bother you — but it will enable it to bring its friends home too! The flap should either

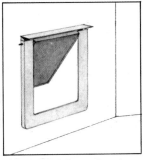

A commercially produced cat-door with a two-part flap which can be opened from either side

be very lightweight or counterbalanced or sprung so that it does not close too rapidly and trap the cat's tail, yet it must be secure enough not to flap in a wind and let in draughts. Several commercial designs are available.

Keep a simple record of important information about your cat and its health:

43

do not rely on memory. An accurate record of innoculations, when symptoms appear, treatments, matings etc will prove invaluable to both you and your vet.

Training
Your kitten will already have been house trained by its mother and you will only need to show it where its litter tray is to encourage it to use it. Other lessons are a matter of patience and firmness. Decide what rules you are going to make, where the cat is to be allowed to go and what it is allowed to do, *and stick to them*. Never allow a cat to do something on one occasion that you will forbid on another. Tone of voice will be an effective reproof, a tap on the nose the strongest blow to which you should resort. Cats are easily frightened by sudden noises and many people believe in striking alongside them with a rolled-up newspaper if, for instance, they jump on a table where they should not be. But, if you adopt this method, you may find that the cat turns it into a game and deliberately jumps up to see you reach for your paper and, having made you do so, will then jump down again.

If you start early enough you may be able to train your cat to walk on a lead. Begin by getting it used to wearing its collar or harness, then attach the lead and get it used to that, putting it on for just a few minutes at a time and allowing the kitten to drag it about. When it has got used to the lead you can begin to hold the other end. Let the kitten lead first, then pull very gently and ask it to go your way – simple words and phrases will be understood more quickly, so say "Come" or "Here". The kitten will probably resist or even sit down. Persist for a few moments then give the kitten a rest before trying again. Keep all lessons down to a few minutes. Eventually the kitten may obey you to avoid the pull of its lead. Do not jerk and give plenty of encouragement when it does the right thing.

Oriental cats are supposed to take to a lead more readily than others. Many Siamese owners wonder how they managed to get that reputation but they probably began their training too late or did not persist with sufficient patience. Many cats will join their owners for a walk without any need for a lead but there are obvious advantages in having a lead-trained cat if you live in a city, or by a busy road, or want to take your cat on a long journey and need to exercise it in strange places.

Cat ailments

Viral diseases
There are two very serious cat diseases: Panleukopaenia (Feline Infectious Enteritis) and Cat Flu, which is the popular name for Feline Viral Rhinotracheitis or Feline Picornavirus Infection, both of which are viral respiratory diseases (also known as Pneumonitis in the United States).

Feline Infectious Enteritis is highly contagious and usually fatal, especially among kittens, but fortunately safe vaccines have been developed which give protection. The cat will probably have been unusually quiet during the two to three days which the germs take to incubate but vomiting, which is often prolonged and severe, is likely to be the first symptom to be noticed. The cat produces froth or fluid stained with bile. There may be diarrhoea and there will be a high temperature and loss of appetite. The cat will appear despondent and although obviously thirsty (the disease produces drastic dehydration) will rarely drink but may sit hunched up over its water bowl. No cure is known for the disease but even if vaccine does not succeed in making the cat totally immune it will give sufficient resistance for the cat to fight the disease and, with careful nursing, to survive. All kittens should be innoculated as soon as possible and regular booster injections given at the dates prescribed.

Both the diseases known as cat flu produce similar symptoms although a veterinarian will recognize the differences between FVR and FPI as they develop. Neither has anything to do with influenza, although the symptoms of high temperature, sneezes, snuffles and dribbling, can be similar. Cats, like us, sneeze for all kinds of minor reasons but if there is a runny nose, excessive salivation and a discharge from the eyes call the vet. Vomiting may also occur and the mouth may become ulcerated. Neither FVR or FPI has as high a mortality rate as FIE and if the cat does not die within the first 48 hours it has a good chance of pulling through if carefully nursed — but it may be a long job with the constant possibility of a relapse. Vaccines against these viruses have been produced but so far the immunity they provide is very short-lived.

If you have reason to suspect that your cat has contracted any of these diseases warn your vet before taking it to his surgery for he may want to make special arrangements, or prefer to visit you at home, to reduce the risk of spreading the infection to other cats. If you have other cats you should keep them away from the infected animal. However, it is no use thinking isolation will protect your cat from these scourges. Even if your pet never goes out and has no contact with other animals you can yourself bring in disease on your shoes and clothing — so take no risks and make sure it is properly innoculated.

Feline Leukemia is another viral condition. It is a cancer of the blood and produces loss of weight and appetite and increasing debility although, since it can affect any of the body's organs, symptoms vary enormously. No cure is known. The disease appears to be transmitted by the mother to her kittens and there is some doubt as to whether cat-to-cat transmission can occur.

Feline Infectious Peritonitis is another virus that attacks young cats. Fever, loss of appetite, lassitude and a swelling of the abdomen are the symptoms and the virus appears to be similar to that which causes leukemia but, although no treatment has been perfected, recovery is possible.

Rabies is now virtually unknown in Britain because strict quarantine laws have controlled entry and all cats leaving quarantine are given anti-rabies injections. Hawaii is the only American state with similar regulations. All cats elsewhere should be given anti-rabies innoculations at three months and boosters each year following. Infection is carried in the saliva of a rabid animal and passed on if it bites or licks a recent wound. A tendency to hide away in the dark followed by growing restlessness and over-reaction to noise are symptoms in the early stages but an infected cat may suddenly and savagely attack anything that crosses its path. There is no treatment. The cat will die within a few days so must be destroyed as soon as possible to prevent the spread of the disease. Do not risk being bitten – throw a piece of sacking or cloth over the cat and trap it beneath a box.

These are the worst diseases which can attack a cat, and you will be extremely unlucky if your cat contracts any of them, but there are many minor complaints that are so common that you are bound to have to cope with them at some time or other.

Common conditions

Fleas However clean the household and careful the rearing, most cats pick up the odd flea at some time or another and even flea-free mothers can sometimes produce a litter of infested kittens. Cat fleas prefer cats and although they might chose a human host if there are no cats available they are unlikely to transfer themselves to you for very long. Treatment is a dusting with flea powder or aerosol spray – but *not* with DDT which is poisonous to cats and can prove fatal in strong concentrations. You may be able to comb fleas out of the coat and crush them between your fingers before they jump. Powder must not get into the cat's eyes or ears. Put the cat on a sheet of newspaper and sprinkle a generous amount of powder on the back of the neck and massage it through the fur down to the skin. Then treat the top of the head, the neck, tail, hindquarters, back, flanks, underparts, legs and toes in that order. Leave the powder for 10 minutes and then brush it vigorously out. Burn the paper. You may need to carry out several treatments before the cat is free.

If your cat roams outdoors and is likely to pick up frequent new infestations from other cats you may like to give it a flea collar. This consists of an impregnated band which kills the fleas when they climb up the body to the head, but they are not very effective on long-haired cats and are disapproved of by some veterinarians because of the possibility of concentrated chemicals being absorbed by the cat.

You will probably be aware of fleas because the cat is scratching itself continually, or you may notice the black specks of flea dirt when you are grooming it. Never neglect them for the build up of irritation and scratching can cause eczema to develop. Fleas lay their eggs in bedding and in cracks and crannies so treat anywhere you think may harbour them to prevent a new infestation when they hatch out. Disposable bedding should be burned.

Ear mites Another common infection, particularly of kittens, is Otodectic mange, or ear canker, caused by a mite which lives in the ear canal. First symptoms are ear scratching and head shaking and on inspection the ear will probably look dirty and there may be a brownish discharge. Treatment with appropriate drops is effective but can be prolonged. Unless you are experienced let the vet carry out the first treatment, cleaning out the discharge and then applying lotion, and follow his instructions for the amount and frequency of later quantities.

Ringworm Not a worm but a fungoid infection that shows as ring-like patches on the skin. This is transferable to humans, especially children, so waste no time in getting your vet to treat it. Most kinds of ringworm produce fluorescence under ultra-violet light. If you have a sun-lamp this could be a quick means of identification but do not expose your cat to ultra-violet radiation for long.

Other external parasites Elderly or sick cats which have difficulty in keeping themselves clean may suffer from maggots which burrow under the skin. They hatch from eggs laid by the bluebottle in wounds or around the anus of cats with serious diarrhoea. If you look after your cat properly it is unlikely to suffer from them. Ticks and lice are seldom found on cats but can be treated in the same way as fleas. The little orange harvest mite found in some places about harvest time can be treated with pyrethrum or swabbed with a weak disinfectant. Cat mange is caused by a mite, *Notoedres cati*, that shows its presence by small bare patches on the ears and face which can spread to cause a serious skin condition. Your vet will treat it with parasiticidal dressings. This mite cannot live on a human host but it can cause unpleasant irritation if it should try to do so.

Internal parasites
Both roundworm and tapeworm can affect cats. They are easily treated with worming pills (but follow your vet's advice on which to use and on the correct dosage). Roundworms are very small and look like thin pieces of string. Symptoms in kittens, which may pick up the worms in their mother's womb, are retarded growth, a blown-out stomach, scurvy skin, vomiting and diarrhoea. If you suspect a roundworm infection take a sample of the cat's faeces to the vet in a clean container. He will easily be able to see the worms under a microscope even if you have not been able to identify them. Tapeworms may not cause any deterioration in a cat's health but they will make it less able to throw off any other infection it may have to fight. Sometimes they cause a cat to lose appetite, sometimes it will eat excessively but lose condition. You are more likely to notice segments of the worm itself, looking like soft grains of rice, either in the faeces or attached to the fur around the anus. Fleas are hosts to the tapeworm in part of its life cycle, so keep it clear of them. Hookworms are much less common, except in hot climates – including the southern United States. They can produce general debility and the most recognizable symptom is bloodstained or tarry diarrhoea. Lungworms are seldom encountered but they produce coughs and wheezes and symptoms suggesting pleurisy and pneumonia. Other parasites are unlikely to be found except for a minute worm which lives in the eye and has been found in certain areas, including the West Coast of the United States. It is easily removed but requires a local anaesthetic so is a job for the vet.

Other diseases
Like humans, the cat can suffer from a number of other diseases and organic malfunctions. It could develop tumours, cysts or warts. Strain upon the kidneys, especially in elderly cats, may produce nephritis. Pneumonia or pleurisy may develop in cases of respiratory infection. An allergy may cause

asthma. Vitamin D deficiency can cause rickets and calcium deficiency, weak bones. Hormonal imbalance may cause hair loss (alopecia). An irritant in the eye may cause conjunctivitis. Cats usually have very strong hearts but occasionally one may suffer a sudden thrombosis. Unlike dogs they rarely suffer badly from arthritic conditions. Unspayed females may develop metritis or pyometritis which are infections of the uterus.

One or two more common conditions affect us all at some time in our lives and the cat is no exception. Constipation and diarrhoea are probably the most likely. Neither should be neglected, for they may be symptoms of something else, but usually they are no cause for alarm. For constipation a small spoonful of liquid paraffin or olive oil (but *not* castor oil) may put it right, or a little uncooked liver will be a good laxative (cooked it is binding). Diarrhoea may be caused by milk in cats who cannot digest it, too much uncooked liver, a change in diet or some unsuitable food. Simply missing a meal sometimes clears it up. A raw beaten egg, if the cat will eat it, or a little kaolin powder mixed with the food, will be binding. If these simple cures do not work and constipation or diarrhoea persist for more than 48 hours they may be the symptoms of something more serious and the cat should be taken to the vet together, in the case of looseness, with a sample of its motion for analysis.

A cat that cries with pain when urinating or seems to strain over its litter tray but passes little urine may be suffering from cystitis, an inflammation of the bladder, which is a fairly common cat complaint. The urine will probably smell strongly of ammonia and may be stained with blood. There is sometimes slight fever and the cat appears very thirsty. It may walk as though the hindquarters are very stiff. If caused by bacterial infection your vet will treat it with antibiotics or sulphonamide drugs and may recommend that you add salt to the cat's food to make it drink more. A chill, bladder stones (cystic calculi), or bladder damage may cause similar symptoms. Male cats with calculi may lick their extruded penis tip and damage its delicate skin. If you can feel the bladder as a hard ball within the abdomen it suggests that no urine is being passed at all and veterinary attention is urgent. Do not squeeze a bladder in this condition – it may burst. Treatment of calculi requires surgery.

Some cats, especially in their later years, suffer from an eczema which may be hormonal or the result of an allergy. It starts as small patches of scabby skin and can spread to the whole body. It is very irritant and the cat can make matters worse by scratching and licking the affected area. Take the cat to the vet. Do not attempt amateur treatments as your diagnosis may be wrong.

A watchful eye

As you get to know your cat you will find that you can recognize its moods and know when it is off-colour just as you do with friends and family. If it seems unhappy or unwell look out for particular symptoms. If you are not absolutely certain that you know the cause and can correct it yourself do not hesitate to consult your vet. He will not feel you are wasting his time.

Since he cannot ask the patient to explain the symptoms you must carefully describe the changes or conditions which you have noticed. When you give any cat its regular grooming make a point of carrying out a routine inspection of its ears, for discharge or parasites, and its eyes, for discharge or conjunctivitis – remember that the appearance of the nictitating membrane is often a danger sign. Check its mouth, for a build up of tartar on the teeth, which can lead to gingivitis; or gingivitis itself – a red inflammation of the gums – which can also be a symptom of more serious disease; for decayed teeth which can cause an abscess; and for sores which could become ulcerous if not treated. Yellow or ivory-coloured gums may indicate anaemia or a liver complaint. They should be pink. So should the tongue. If its tip is bright red this may indicate a viral infection. Do not forget to look at the paws for damaged pads, broken claws and thorns and splinters all of which can lead to trouble if ignored.

Accidents and injuries
Cats, especially those in towns, are threatened more by mishaps than by disease. Road accidents account for most of the broken limbs (if the damage is not worse) that have to be treated and abscesses developing from wounds gained in a fight account for another big proportion of the cases seen by veterinarians. Do not try to treat a cat injured in a road accident yourself, unless you see that it is losing a lot of blood and you know where and how to apply a tourniquet. A folded handkerchief or pad of cotton wool bound over a wound should be sufficient to stem the loss of blood in a minor injury. Get it to a vet or a vet to it straight away. Gently lift the injured animal on to a coat or rug – disturb its position as little as possible in case you cause further internal injury. Wear gloves if you have them for in its pain it may bite or maul anyone who touches it. Then lower the cat, on the rug, into a box or basket. Keep it warm and move it as little as possible on its way to the vet. You may not feel that you have done much to alleviate its agony but you have prevented it from injuring itself further or dragging itself away to die.

If your cat is limping and you think it may have broken a bone you can test for a broken limb by placing the cat gently on a table and comparing the suspected limb with its partner. Do they look a different length? Do they hang differently? Get an assistant to hold the cat over a table by the scruff of its neck with one hand and to take its weight on the other hand held beneath its chest. If you think a hind leg is injured raise the chest slightly so that the cat's weight is taken at its rear. Is all the weight taken on one hind leg and does the cat flinch as the suspected leg touches the table? If you think a front leg may be fractured move the cat towards the edge of the table. Most cats will instinctively reach out for the edge and if it pulls itself forward with the suspect leg you can be reasonably sure that it is not broken.

Bites and scratches or cuts from glass or tin cans should be cleaned with a weak antiseptic to prevent infection. Never use carbolic or any preparation containing coal tar or phenol which will harm cats. If bleeding persists a tourniquet may be necessary and if a gash is large it will probably require stitching by your vet. Cats' wounds usually heal very rapidly and light ones will need little more attention. More serious are wounds which you do not notice until some time after they have been sustained. A cat will probably slink away after a fight, literally to lick its wounds, and they may begin to fester before you see them. Do not treat them with antiseptic. Salt water or disinfectant will be better. Puncture wounds, where teeth or claws have penetrated deep but left only a small hole on the skin, may heal on the surface leaving the wound beneath infected so that an abscess develops. The pus will need drawing out with a cloth soaked in warm, salted water. Squeeze out the cloth and apply it while hot to the swelling. Repeat the operation as soon as it begins to cool. After 10 or 15 minutes dry the skin and then give the same treatment again four or five hours later. Abscesses on the ears, the neck, joints and the tail are very dangerous and should be treated by your vet. Ask his advice in any case for he may wish to give a shot of penicillin as a safety measure. Continue bathing even after the abscess bursts for you must be sure that all the poison has been removed or another abscess will develop after the top skin has healed. After the abscess has burst add hydrogen peroxide to the bathing water. This will help to remove the pus and to diminish the smell, which in turn may also lessen the cat's instinctive reaction to lick the sore.

Cats are great fly catchers and when they are young may try to tackle a bee or a wasp — they learn not to by experience as they get older. Stings near the eyes or in the mouth, where they hamper breathing, should be treated by your vet but otherwise they rarely do much harm although stings on the lips or chin may bring up big swellings. Pull the sting out with your nails or with tweezers, rub on a little antihistamine ointment if you have it, and all should be well.

Household accidents

Train your cat not to jump on to stoves even when they are cold — for it will have no means of knowing when a surface is hot and burned paw pads are extremely painful. If you do have such an accident smother the paws with vaseline and then wrap soft cloth around them. That will ease the pain and keep out the air. Do not try to bandage them. Most cats soon learn the normal hazards of fires and candle flames and a little singed fur or a whisker or two sacrificed to experience will not do them any harm. Nevertheless, for your own safety do not leave open fires unscreened when you are not at home.

Cats more frequently get scalded than burned, and it is usually their owner's fault, a pan handle having been knocked or an overfilled kettle suddenly spurting boiling water. Bad scalds must be treated by a vet, very minor ones may be eased by covering the area with vaseline or olive oil. If a layer of skin comes off leaving a bare patch this needs especially careful treatment. Once the fur has dried a scald may not be noticed. If there are signs of something having been spilt and your cat seems to be in pain when you stroke it this could be the reason.

Corrosive substances can be as dangerous as fire. Not only acids and caustic substances but paraffin (kerosene), tar, creosote, wood seals, most paints and paint thinners – and their fumes – are all harmful to cats. Keep them where it is impossible for the cat to get and keep all animals well away while you are using them and while they are still wet. A battery acid or petroleum spill on the garage floor or a newly creosoted garden fence are typical dangers. They may act on the skin or, if only picked up on the fur, burn the cat's tongue and be swallowed when the cat tries to clean itself.

Treat acid by pushing the cat into a bucket of water in which you have mixed a generous amount of sodium bicarbonate. Treat caustic burns by using boracic acid instead of sodium bicarbonate. Protect your hands from burns with rubber gloves. If you do not know what caused the burn, dip the cat in plain water to dilute the substance then wrap it in a blanket and rush it to the vet. The cat won't like it so be prepared for a fight. Creosote can be removed by olive oil or medicinal paraffin. Weak washing-up liquid will remove kerosene – but rinse it off well afterwards. Do not use turpentine or other solvents to remove paint. Wipe it off, clip the fur if necessary. Do not take risks. Get the cat to the vet to make sure all is well.

Slivers of glass, thorns or wood splinters may become imbedded in the paws. If your cat is limping this may be the cause. Gentle pressure and a pair of tweezers will get them out if they still protrude. You will need someone else to control the cat. Bathe the wound afterwards with mild antiseptic and make sure that no dirt has been left in it. If the wound has already become infected you would do better to leave it to your vet.

Sewing needles can fall out of the workbox unnoticed and stick into the cat. Provided they have not broken off they are comparatively easy to remove and the wound will not be serious. If there was a thread of cotton attached a cat may have been playing with it and the needle become lodged in its mouth. Even this is no cause for alarm and if you are calm and do not panic you may be able to remove it yourself holding the mouth open as though you were giving a pill (see below) and gripping the needle with a pair of pliers. If you have any doubts of your ability to extract it take the cat to the vet. If it is wedged it will do little more damage on the way there and you might do a great deal through your clumsiness. If you think your cat may have swallowed a needle the first action should be an X-ray at the vet's. Cats love to play with thread and string so be careful to ensure that needles are always securely put away.

Sometimes a cat will swallow a length of string. It will almost certainly pass safely through but the cat may end up with a piece trailing from its behind. If this happens do not tug on the string. With someone else holding the cat, and making sure that you can really see what you are doing, try to pull it very gently. If there is any resistance leave it to find its own way out and do not risk pulling the lining of the rectum with it. If a long piece is hanging out cut it (taking care not to tug as you do so) to not more than an inch and a half so that it will not be long enough for the cat to play with and cause injury to itself. If it does not pass through soon the vet should be consulted.

Electric shock

It is not often that cats bite through electricity cables but train your cat not to play with them and avoid unnecessary trailing wires in the house. If a cat bites through the insulation it may well be unable to release itself from the cable. Switch the current off before you do anything else. The shock may have made the cat urinate so watch your step – urine is a good conductor of electricity. If you cannot turn the current off wear rubber gloves or rubber boots to insulate yourself before you try to pull the cat away and make sure that you make no other contact which could make an earth or ground connection. Once the cat is clear you can apply artificial respiration. If possible do this while someone else drives you to the vet. There is a risk of heart failure and veterinary attention is urgent.

Poisons

Never leave poisonous substances where they are accessible to cats and that includes DDT, carbolic-based disinfectants, and the plethora of weed-killers, pesticides and household chemicals which we all make use of today. Read labels and find out the antidotes to any poisons you keep around the house and stock them too. With so many garden and agricultural chemicals in use a cat may easily eat a chemically poisoned mouse, bird or fly, even if it does not take a poison direct. Toadstools and other natural poisons are as dangerous for cats as for humans; laurel, philodendron and dieffenbachia plants are also poisonous. If you know that poisons are in use in the neighbourhood for rodent control or some other purpose discover what they are, what symptoms they produce and what antidote should be used. Your local health officer may be able to tell you. Keep a mixture of a "universal antidote" – your local pharmacy will make one up. This usually consists of magnesium oxide, charcoal and tannic acid and you can make your own in an emergency from milk of magnesia, burnt toast and strong tea. This mix is said to be able to absorb as much as 15 times its own weight of coal-tar poison and more than a 100 times its own weight of strychnine. A kitten should be given at least one and preferably two tablespoonfuls and a grown cat should be made to swallow twice that quantity.

It is unlikely that you will actually see a cat eat a poison so it will be such symptoms as vomiting, diarrhoea, nervous twitches and fits, loss of consciousness and obvious stomach pains which attract your attention. They could all be symptoms of other things as well. If you firmly believe that your cat has been poisoned give the right antidote if you know it, failing that the universal mixture or, as a last resort make it vomit (but *not* if its mouth is burned), by giving hydrogen peroxide diluted in 12 times the quantity of water. Then get it to the vet as soon as possible.

Nursing the sick cat

A sick cat needs to be kept comfortable and clean, to be reassured of your affection and to be given sufficient attention to encourage it to get well, but it should not be fussed over for it will probably need plenty of sleep to build up its strength. Make a comfortable bed with old blankets and newspaper and place it somewhere quiet and warm, away from bright light and free from draughts. A hot water bottle (frequently refilled to make sure it is always warm) will also help. Change the bedding if it gets soiled. Make sure there is fresh drinking water close by and put the litter tray within easy reach. Elderly invalids and very sick cats may need carrying to their litter tray two or three times a day and cleaning up a little after they have used it.

Always follow your vet's instructions carefully. If you are not absolutely sure what you are supposed to do get him to repeat them and explain anything you do not understand, he would much rather you do that than risk being misinterpreted. Carefully note all changes and developments in the cat's behaviour and condition, however insignificant they seem, so that you can report them accurately to your vet. Even if you think the cat is fully recovered keep up treatment or you may risk a relapse. Stop only when your vet tells you to stop.

All sick cats will appreciate a little extra grooming and it will help with their morale. Bathe their eyes and clean their nose with warm salt water, if they seem to need it. If nose leather or lips become cracked wipe them with a little cod liver oil. Keep to the diet your vet recommends. If a cat refuses to eat spoil it with some of its favourite foods (if they are not forbidden) to whet its appetite. If you know that your cat is to be given an anaesthetic do not feed it the night before (or for whatever period your vet requires).

Pills and medicines
Love and attention are needed with any illness but they will not cure the patient on their own. Some drugs will be administered by injection either

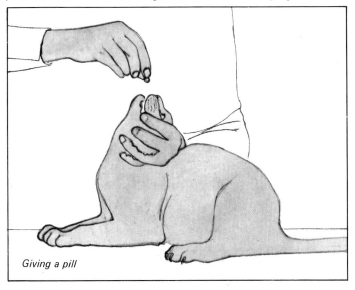

Giving a pill

into the muscle tissue or into the veins, but those to be given at home will usually be powders, pills or liquid medicines. Powders are the easiest to give, you simply mix them with the cat's food. If the cat *refuses* to eat it, rejecting several meals, the vet will have to try some other way. Some cats take pills easily, many do not. Until you gain experience you may find you need an assistant to hold the cat while you administer them. The assistant should hold the patient's forelegs and slightly support the cat's rear while you hold the cat's head from above much as you might hold a ball. Move the skull upwards and backwards, squeezing gently with the fingers on either side of the mouth. Hold the pill in the other hand and with one finger press the lower jaw down. Don't put your finger between the cat's teeth but press on the gum to hold the mouth open while you drop the tablet to the back of the tongue. Immediately hold the mouth shut and stroke the throat until you are quite sure that cat has swallowed the pill. Do not release the cat until it has licked its lips for it may be holding the pill in its mouth ready to spit it out as soon as your back is turned. Some pills tend to froth in the mouth if not swallowed, which the cat will find very unpleasant, so if it has not gone down let the cat spit it out and try again. With experience you will be able to give a pill on your own. You can either hold the cat on a table or cradle it on its back to reduce its resistance.

Liquid medicine can be given by spoon or dropper on to the back of the tongue in a similar way. If it is a large dose do it in several stages so that there is no risk of making the cat choke and cough it out. Another method is to hold the cat's head still and horizontal while you pull a pouch of skin away from the lower jaw and pour or squirt the medicine in the gap between the teeth. In both cases hold the mouth closed and stroke the throat.

If a medicine or pill which is not intended to be an emetic produces vomiting, and it is not simply the cat refusing to swallow, inform your vet for it may mean that your cat is allergic to that particular drug.

Artificial respiration
Lay the cat on its side and press gently on its chest, release the pressure and apply it again rhythmically with about four seconds between each movement. Alternatively you may take the cat's mouth in your own and apply mouth-to-mouth resuscitation.

Bandaging
Because cat's flesh heals so rapidly there is little need to bandage slight wounds unless you have had to treat them with an ointment which it would be dangerous for the cat to lick, or if the cat persists in licking them and delaying healing. You may also have to bandage a cat's paws to stop it scratching an irritant area which can soon become raw and torn. If a cat needs bandaging, it needs bandaging well for otherwise it will claw or bite the bandage off.

Always lay the bandage on flat and evenly. Wrap it firmly but not so tightly that it interferes with the circulation. Do not tie the ends or secure them with a safety pin. Instead always use sticking plaster which should

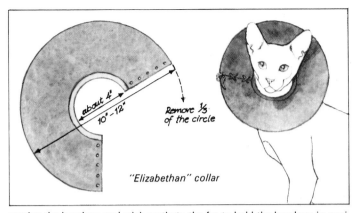

about 4"

10' - 12'

Remove ⅓ of the circle

"Elizabethan" collar

overlap the bandage and stick partly to the fur to hold the bandage in position. Ordinary gauze and crêpe bandages can be used and a tubular bandage will prove an asset when bandaging the paws to stop scratching. An "Elizabethan" collar made of card will prevent a cat from licking and worrying wounds or from scratching sore eyes or ears. Make one from a circle of card (a large breakfast cereal pack flattened out will serve) about 12 ins in diameter. Cut away an arc of about one third of the circle and remove a smaller circle about 4 ins across. Try this around the cat's neck and make any necessary adjustments then make holes along the overlapping edges and tape the inner edge with sticking plaster so that it does not chafe the cat's neck. Put the collar on the cat and lace the edges together, tying a bow so that the collar can be easily removed but without leaving loose ends which the cat could pull upon. You will have to take the collar off for the cat to feed and wash itself — but keep watch to see that it does not do the very things the collar is supposed to prevent. Never let a cat wearing an Elizabethan collar out of doors for it will restrict its field of vision and may lead to accidents and make it very vulnerable to attack.

Taking a cat's temperature

The temperature of cats is taken by inserting an heavy glass thermometer up the rectum. The thin thermometer used for humans is too fragile and should not be used. The thermometer must be greased and inserted gently, it should be rotated but *not* pushed. Remember to remove it gently too. The cat will not like the operation so be calm and reassuring and have someone else hold the cat's shoulders and front feet firmly while you support the abdomen with one hand and insert the thermometer with the other. If you have any doubt of your ability to do it properly do not take risks — and never take a cat's temperature unnecessarily.

A cat's normal temperature is about 101.5°F (38.5°C). A temperature over 102.8°F suggests some kind of infection and any reading beyond 100.5°F and 102°F (38°C and 39°C) means that you should consult your vet.

Boarding catteries

Some cats which are particularly person-orientated will enjoy a trip away, particularly if it is to a regular weekend or vacation home with which they can become familiar. For shortish journeys they need only their basket; for longer ones take a litter tray along or be prepared to stop to let the cat relieve itself, in which case it must, of course, be kept on a lead. More often it will be better to arrange for someone else to care for the cat while you are away. Whoever you leave in charge give them clear instructions or you may return to find an overfed and spoiled cat who is not very keen on returning to normal discipline. Ideally have someone the cat knows come to stay. Alternatively, ask a friend or neighbour to come in and deal with the food and litter tray, *and give the cat a little attention*. A confident outdoor cat may even get used to going next door for dinner while you are away but you may run the risk of it deciding that they offer a better home. If there is no one you can trust to look after your cat properly and you have to be away then you must leave it in a cattery. In Britain, boarding catteries have to be registered and are supposed to conform to certain standards but you would always be wise to inspect a cattery before deciding to leave your cat in its charge for the first time. If it is staying for a long visit there should be outdoor run which is properly enclosed so that there can be no contact with other cats or animals. There should be a stone or concrete floor which is easier to disinfect. Occasional outbreaks of infection occur in the best-run catteries but these provisions will reduce the risk. The housing should be dry and draught free but with adequate light and ventilation and, when necessary, a safe form of heating. The cattery owner will expect you to have certificates to prove that the cat is immunized against FIE so check that its booster injections are up to date. Think twice about a cattery which does not insist on this. If it is allowed, leave a favourite cushion or toy and give a written note of any special diet. Do not expect a cattery to follow a fussy diet — only one that is medically necessary. Indeed you may find a fussy cat cured of its fads when you get back from your trip.

Never leave a sick or convalescent cat in kennels unless it is absolutely unavoidable, and then explain the situation to the owner when you make the arrangements. If you are forced to leave a sick cat ask your vet to help you find accommodation. Elderly cats who are used to a regular stay in kennels can be boarded out without undue concern but the change may prove too much for an ageing cat which has never had the experience.

Moving house

Make provision well in advance for the cat to have a comfortable journey without being able to get lost. When you reach your destination do not let it run free at first but keep it indoors for a few days to let it identify with its new home. If you are moving from a home in the country to a city apartment many floors up and the cat is used to an unrestricted outdoor life, it may be kinder to ask the new occupants of your house to take it or have it adopted by neighbours that it already knows.

Travel tips
For a long journey do not feed or give liquids for five or six hours beforehand and you will reduce toilet problems. For journeys over 24 hours give one meal on the trip. On a short trip the cat will enjoy being able to see out but a covered basket will encourage it to sleep on a long one. However, make sure the cover does not interfere with ventilation. If a cat is very nervous your veterinarian may agree to prescribe a tranquillizer – but keep exactly to the dose he recommends. Many cats, especially Siamese, will chatter a great deal at the beginning of a journey. This is more likely to be out of interest and excitement than from fear but join in the conversation and you will reassure it.

If you send a cat by rail make sure that there is someone to meet it at the station of arrival. Cats usually make good sailors and may enjoy a trip by sea – there have always been ship's cats after all. Airlines often have their own rules and supply a special container. If you are travelling with a cat check on the regulations first.

Quarantine
To restrict the spread of rabies and other dangerous diseases the United Kingdom, Australia and Eire and the state of Hawaii insist that all live-stock which might carry them must spend six months in quarantine following arrival in the country. This can put a great strain on both the cat and its owners. If you are going to move permanently to those countries it may be worthwhile. If you are only visiting, leave your cat behind unless you are going on to another country after only a very brief stay in which case it may be better to have the cat in quarantine and soon reunited with you rather than to leave it for a longer stay in kennels elsewhere. The other states of the USA insist on a certificate of health for all imported cats.

Cats and the law
There is no international agreement on the protection of cats and the responsibilities of cat owners. In Britain, for instance, the cat is untaxed but is protected by the Acts protecting all animals from cruelty and abandon-ment. Anyone who causes damage to a cat through cruelty or injury is liable to compensate its owner, and any owner who fails to protect their cat from cruelty or causes cruelty by neglect is liable to a fine or imprison-ment or both. Anyone performing an operation on a cat without due care and humanity or permitting such an operation to be performed on a cat in their charge can be similarly punished. Nevertheless, because it is classed as a wild animal there is no requirement to report a road accident involving a cat and British owners are not held responsible for their cats' misdeeds even if they kill a neighbour's bird or dig up his prize plants.

In the United States, the Commonwealth and many other countries the cat is given some protection from cruelty. In the USA exact legislation varies from state to state, and even from borough to borough. At Saddle Brook,

New Jersey, cats must be licensed and wear a bell. In New York State any cat found hunting or killing birds may be humanely destroyed by anyone over 21 with a hunting licence.

Find out if there is any special legislation that applies to your locality. If you have a rented home your lease may require you to get special permission, or even forbid you to keep a cat.

Cat Protection Societies

The general animal welfare organizations such as the RSPCA, the ASPCA and the Humane Society work for the better treatment of cats, along with other animals, bringing prosecutions for cruelty and educating the public in their attitude to their pets. Organizations such as the Blue Cross and the PDSA provide free or inexpensive treatment and if you have a veterinary training college in your locality you will almost certainly find that they run a free clinic too. Many vets devote part of their time to working in these clinics and some even set aside special times in their own practices to run free clinics so there is no reason why lack of money should stop a cat from being properly treated.

RAISING KITTENS

Female cats usually reach sexual maturity between five and nine months old. They may develop an obsessive need to give and to receive more than their usual ration of affection. They will rub themselves against people and things, they may roll in an abandoned fashion on their backs, they may shiver with excitement or rush around quite wildly. They may cry out as though they were being tortured. Many an owner has taken their cat to the vet with symptoms such as these thinking that she must be seriously sick. She is not. She is on heat.

There are some females who scarcely show these symptoms at all – or perhaps there are just some very unobservant owners. There are others, particularly Siamese, who have the neighbourhood sending for the police to stop you murdering your spouse unless you issue warning of what the painful howls really mean. Most cats are somewhere in between. Their calls and the special odour which they produce during oestrus will inform tom cats for miles around that they are ready for mating.

The frequency with which a cat comes on heat varies considerably from cat to cat and location, time of year, weather and environment may all affect the pattern. Orientals seem to come in season particularly frequently and with little regard to the calendar. Laboratory studies suggest that females come on heat every two or three weeks during January and February and then again in June and July but at less frequent intervals. However, the experience of millions of cat owners makes such hard and fast statements debatable. Heat may last as little as three days if there is a male available and sometimes more than a fortnight if there is not. A cat may not be very ready to accept a tom during its first heat and in any case it is better to wait until a cat is older before it has to raise a litter: there is plenty of time, queens (entire females) have been known to produce kittens at 20 years of age.

If you hope to breed from a queen but feel she is too young or there is some reason not to do so at present such as an impending move or holiday, keep the cat indoors. You may have to watch her closely for the instinct to mate is very strong and leaving a window or any likely exit open must be avoided. If she is an outdoor cat not trained to a litter tray, or the need for access for other cats means that you cannot keep her in, there are feline pills which will prevent her coming on heat. Although the occasional use of the drug does not have any known side effects, it is obviously better not to interfere with the natural cycle and it is preferable to have the cat spayed than to continue administering a pill. Similarly, a cat should not persistently be prevented from mating or serious disorders of the urino-genital system may develop.

Males take longer to reach maturity and although they may be able to mate at eight months some are well over a year before they can sire a litter. This may be related to the time of year that they were born: under natural conditions some seasons are less suitable for rearing young. However, the male cat has no heat cycle and once he starts to mate is sexually active whenever he gets the chance.

If you have a pedigree male that you want to keep as a stud you will need to build him outdoor quarters as the pungent smell of his spray will make it impossible to keep a full male indoors. You need warm sleeping quarters with separate accommodation for queens, so that they can take some time to get acquainted before the actual mating, and a good-sized netted run for exercise. If you live in the country you may be able to let him have several hours' free exercise each day. A young male should not be used as a stud until it is a year old and its first mating should be with an experienced queen if possible. For the first few months he should only be mated once or twice. Some mature toms manage a queen a day but to allow time for the two cats to get to know each other and for several matings to take place most breeders would only recommend two or three matings a week and would have a two to four-month non-breeding season for the tom to rest. If you are not able to find a regular supply of queens you may find the sexually deprived male will become neurotic so do not keep a stud tom unless you are prepared to organize the whole thing in a professional way.

A form of sex-play often occurs in pre-pubescent kittens. Even in females it follows adult male behaviour involving neck biting, mounting and similar activities. In adults, homosexual behaviour is not unusual. It is more

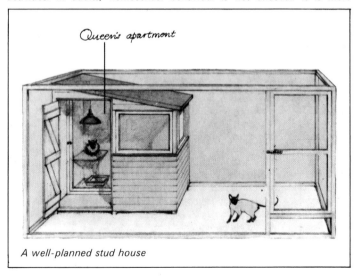

A well-planned stud house

common among males but females in the same household may sometimes mount a frustrated queen on heat.

A whole female who is allowed out of doors when on heat will usually have no difficulty in attracting a mate. In fact all the toms of the neighbourhood will probably vie for her attentions. They may do battle to gain the right to woo her but the victor will not necessarily win her. Queens sometimes have quite clear ideas on whom they will take as a mate. It is not necessarily the biggest and strongest and she may even mate with a weaker tom while the champions fight it out. The female may play very hard to get — and if she is a virgin it may take considerable effort and patience on the part of the tom. Indeed she may well turn on him and many queens attack the male when mating is completed. In natural conditions a cat may be mated by one tom after another and, if she rejects one may find another tom upon her before she can resist. In arranged stud matings cats do sometimes reject a particular tom entirely. On other occasions a real affection seems to develop and they will happily curl up together. The tom is rarely choosy and the free-ranging male will seek out any receptive female over a wide area.

Arranging a meeting
Once you let a calling queen out of doors you can have little control over her matings but in taking your queen to a pedigree stud you will be able to select one that has the characteristics and temperament you need to produce the best possible kittens. Even if you have no interest in competitive showing you will want happy, healthy kittens without defects so will look for a strong strain. At the same time try to compensate for any faults in your own cat by choosing a stud which has particularly good qualities where she is weak. Very closely related cats are sometimes mated to duplicate their good points. This fixes type more quickly than any other method but it also fixes undesirable qualities. Such close mating is known as in-breeding. Line-breeding uses cats from the same ancestry to achieve similar results and is usual when there is a particularly fine forbear whose characteristics it is wished to preserve. Out-breeding is the opposite of in-breeding and is the way in which new traits are introduced into a strain. As with any carefully developed stock the selection of breeding partners is a very scientific business and if you intend to take breeding seriously you should seek professional help. Consult the breeder from whom you originally got your cat, attend local cat shows and find out from local cat clubs which breeders in the locality have suitable toms. In Britain, the Governing Council of the Cat Fancy publishes a list of owners who offer pedigree male cats for stud. North American owners may find one advertised in *Cats Magazine*.

When your queen comes on heat you will need to take action rapidly so make provisional arrangements well beforehand. The stud owner will usually charge a fee which includes boarding and food and it is usual for a free service to be given if the queen does not conceive, but there is no obligation to offer this. Sometimes the owner may expect to have a choice of kittens from the litter and this may be suggested in lieu of a stud fee. They will certainly insist that your cat is in good health and is up to date with all the usual innoculations. This is to protect both the stud and your own animal from infection.

A queen is usually at her most receptive on the third day of heat and many breeders think that this is also the most successful time for conception. Contact the stud owner as soon as your cat comes on heat. If the tom you want already has a queen with him you may have to use a different tom. Most breeders prefer the queen to spend a little time in the stud house for the cats to get acquainted and will not attempt a mating until the second day of her stay. At least two matings will be given, and probably more, before you collect the queen.

Whether courtship is protracted or brief depends upon the individual cats. Sometimes a well-tempered female, when bred with a gentle tom, displays none of the initial rejection pattern that is customary and they are behaving like a honeymoon couple almost as soon as they meet. More often the male, who will circle the female sniffing her rear quarters and talking to her, will be warned off with spits, growls and slaps if he comes too close. When she is not making him keep his distance she will roll on her back, crouch, tread and call back. Eventually she will be prepared to accept the tom, and only then will he attempt copulation – unless he is very inexperienced.

The queen will crouch excitedly, with her head down and her hindquarters in the air, while the tom takes the loose skin on the back of her neck in his teeth and mounts her from behind, first with his forelegs and then with his hindlegs as well. Both cats tread up and down with their hind legs and the tom begins to lunge forward with his pelvis. He returns his hindlegs to the ground and the queen moves herself to balance his action and facilitate the entrance of his penis. It is not an easy procedure and the female may become so irritated and frustrated that she breaks away from the tom and the process has to be repeated, sometimes several times.

When intromission eventually takes place ejaculation is rapid and it is all over in a matter of seconds. The cat's penis, unlike that of other animals, is covered with short barbed spines which develop from the age of about three and a half months if it has not been previously castrated. On withdrawal, these barbs apparently hurt the queen for she usually makes a loud cry and often turns on the tom. She then rolls on her back. This is believed to play some part in the process of fertilization.

Pay the stud fee when you collect your cat and make sure that the stud owner gives you a copy of his cat's pedigree before you go – if you have not previously been given it. In the United States matings without documentation are sometimes given for a lower fee. Make sure all the arrangements are agreed *before* you take your cat to the stud.

The Pregnant Queen
Keep your cat away from other toms until you are sure she is off heat – if the mating has not been successful you could accidentally land yourself with a mongrel litter, or, since cats can conceive by different fathers in the same litter, you might add to those already conceived. Your queen will not require any special attention but discourage her from being over-active for

a few days. There will be no sign that she is pregnant for about three weeks, then you may notice that her nipples look redder than usual and 10 days or so later they may begin to swell. Experienced breeders can even feel the kittens in her womb but do not risk damage by squeezing her. Get your vet to confirm whether she is actually carrying a litter.

When the pregnant cat begins to ask for more food give it to her and to ensure that she has the extra vitamins and minerals which she needs give a supplement: your vet will probably recommend a powder form which can be mixed with her food. It is particularly important that she gets calcium and vitamin D but some breeders are careful to control the amount of food and calcium to prevent the formation of very large kittens which might be difficult to deliver.

The cat's gestation period is usually from 63 to 65 days. Sometimes a cat will delay the birth if her owner is away from home and Siamese in particular may be overdue. Naturally there are some cases when a birth is premature. It is always wise to take your cat for a check-up a week or so before the kittens are due to make sure that all is going well and particularly so when it is a cat's first pregnancy.

As her time approaches the mother-to-be will show signs of wanting to make a nest. Prepare a large box for her, lining it with newspaper, and put it in a warm, dark corner away from household activities. Put her in it occasionally and if she rejects this as a place to have her kittens note where she seems to favour and put the box there if it is not too unsuitable. If you do not provide somewhere for kittening you may find that she will choose an awkward corner in a cupboard where you cannot get to help her or simply use your bed.

Birth

Most cats can cope with birth without any human assistance but some will prefer company. Usually you will know when her time is close by increased displays of affection, traces of milk on the nipples or possibly a slight discharge from the vagina, and she will probably alternate scratching with squatting. Add a blanket to the paper which she will have torn up in the kittening box and a towel to keep it clean. If you are present at the time of birth check that the delivery of each kitten is followed by the expulsion of the placenta. A placenta retained inside the cat could lead to serious infection later. The mother will break the sac which contains the kitten, clean up the kitten, bite through the umbilical cord and eat the placenta. If the kittens arrive too fast for the mother to carry all this out, or if for any other reason she seems unable to cope, you will have to help so be ready with a rough towel, a wrapped hot water bottle and paper tissues and give your hands and nails a thorough scrub. You can tear open the sac with your fingers and clean the kitten with the towel, taking care that its mouth is not blocked with mucus. A vigorous rubbing is usually sufficient to start the kitten breathing, if it is not apply artificial respiration. To sever the umbilical cord grip it close to the kitten's body with the thumb and finger of one hand, thus ensuring that you do not tug upon it; about three inches along the cord grip it with the other hand pressing the thumb nail against the first finger and rubbing it to and fro until it separates. If a placenta does not come completely away draw it out with a finger and thumb. If a breech delivery seems to be wedged (and since they can take from three minutes up to half an hour do not panic), grip the protruding part of the kitten firmly with a piece of clean towel and help to ease it out as the mother strains. The hot water bottle will help to keep the new-born kittens warm. But do not let it go cold.

A pre-natal check up with the vet will have given warning if a Caesarean delivery is likely to be necessary but particularly in cases of first pregnancy warn your vet when the litter is expected so that he can be prepared if there should be an emergency. Your vet may be able to tell you how many kittens to expect. Litters are usually about four to six but single kittens are not uncommon and litters of over a dozen have been known. If there is a very large litter the mother may not be able to rear them all successfully and you should ask your vet's advice on how many she should be allowed to raise herself. Alternatively, it may be possible simply to supplement her efforts by feeding them by hand in rotation to relieve demand on her milk and by assisting in keeping them clean.

Once all the litter has been born your cat will need a good rest. Make sure food, fresh water – and her litter tray – are near to hand so that she does not have to leave her kittens for long to reach them.

The new-born kitten
When they are born the kittens' eyes are closed and will not open until they are about nine days old. They use their sense of smell and, to a lesser extent, that of touch to find their mother's nipples and are able to suckle, if she will let them, within minutes of birth. They often develop a preference for a particular nipple and this helps to eliminate squabbles at feeding time. Although most litters grow rapidly during their early weeks they must be watched for any indication that the kittens are not gaining weight and the mother checked to see that she is not building up surplus milk. Sometimes a litter of apparently healthy kittens suddenly stops suckling, rapidly weakens and dies. This occurrence is known to veterinarians as the "fading kitten syndrome" but they do not understand why it happens. Attempts to save the kittens are rarely successful. The mother cat continues to produce milk which creates painful pressure in the mammary glands and serious problems may develop if she is not given the correct attention so consult your vet.

It is often easier to tell the sex of a kitten when it is very young than when its fur has grown. The male's genitals are further from the anus than those of the female but there is little other noticeable difference. If you have a mixed litter it should not be too difficult to judge.

Even at five days old kittens are able to find their way back to the nest from short distances away but it is not until they are about three weeks old and their eyes have been open for nearly two weeks that they begin to use their sight as a major means of orientation and wander further from the nest.

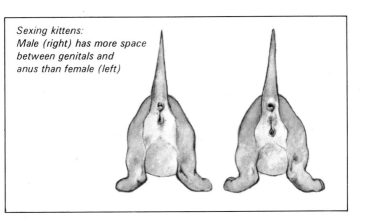

*Sexing kittens:
Male (right) has more space
between genitals and
anus than female (left)*

About this time they may begin to take an interest in their mother's food and will perhaps imitate her and try to lap up some of it. A few days after you notice this try offering them evaporated milk or strongly-made powdered milk and if they lap it up mix in a little cooked baby cereal. Do not overdo it. A teaspoonful a day is quite enough to begin with and you can gradually increase it after they have been taking it for a week. They are still taking their nourishment from their mother and this is only the beginning of the weaning process. Continue the mother's vitamin and calcium supplement through the whole of the suckling period as it will help her to produce the milk the kittens need.

Gradually the kittens will take more food and rely less on their mother. From three weeks they will be suckling at their choice rather than at their mother's instigation and their mother will begin to give them slightly less attention. If they show no sign at all of lapping try offering a drop of milk on the end of a clean finger or dab some on their noses to prompt their licking.

From four weeks old the kittens will begin to get their first set of teeth and at four and a half weeks you can begin to offer a little scraped or minced raw beef and some lightly scrambled eggs. At six weeks old they should be having five or six small snacks every day, two or three of them of meat, and suckling on their mother only at bedtime. If they persistently demand her nipples you must keep them away from her or weaning may be postponed indefinitely. Take the opportunity to give her some attention and a little respite from the kittens' demands.

Small kittens have tiny stomachs so it is essential that they are fed little and often. As they grow their meals can become larger and less frequent, but do not give them more than they can clean off the dish at a sitting or you may encourage them to overeat. At eight weeks they should be down to four meals a day and soon after to three but they will not be ready to manage on a single meal until they are at least six months old. Even then many people will prefer to feed two meals, breakfast and an evening meal. Always keep fresh drinking water available throughout the cat's life. Kittens, and many adult cats, especially orientals, do not enjoy cow's milk which they find difficult to digest, but even if they like it they will still need plenty of water.

Orphan Kittens

There is sometimes an untypical mother who abandons, or even attacks, her offspring. She may also reject the weakest of the litter because they have defects which make them unlikely to survive or because she simply has not got sufficient milk to raise them all. A tragic accident at the birth or sickness may deprive the young ones of their mother or make her too weak to rear them. In all these cases the kittens must be fostered or hand-reared if they are to survive.

The easiest and probably the most successful method is to find another female who has just lost a kitten or has surplus milk and can cope with an addition to her own litter. Many ruses have been tried to encourage a foster mother to accept an orphan as one of her own. If a mare or ewe has lost a foal or lamb the skin of the dead animal put over the orphan has successfully done the trick. This is scarcely possible with cats but if you rub the kitten with a little milk gently squeezed from the foster mother, this will also give an odour which makes it seem like one of her own. Urine may also be used and is a method which can be adopted to make an older animal accept a new young member of the household. It helps if the foster mother is not allowed to nurse for some hours before the orphan is introduced to her. The pressure of the milk on her mammary glands causes some discomfort and in the relief at its release the mother will be less critical of the agent responsible. Having once suckled the orphan it is unlikely that the foster mother will then reject it.

If there is no suitable cat available you may be able to persuade a bitch or some other animal in milk to accept an orphan, but failing that you will either have to have the kitten or kittens destroyed or be the foster mother yourself. It is not a job to take on lightly. You must take on *all* the mother's duties: not only keeping them nourished but keeping them warm and clean.

The first requirement is a warm and draught-free environment. Most losses among orphans are due to their being too cold. There are many views as to what the ideal temperature pattern should be, but as a general guide for the first day they need to be kept at about 90°F (32°C). For the next four or five days 85°F (29°C) and at two weeks as low as 70°F (21°C). The best way of keeping them warm is to rig up an incubator.

The easiest form is a 40-watt bulb suspended above a wooden box. Keep the bulb at least six inches away from the kittens and as they get older reduce the temperature by raising the height of the bulb. The light may disturb the kittens and a lamp beneath the box will give off plenty of warmth without that problem, although the temperature will be harder to control. Make sure that there is plenty of ventilation so that there is no risk of fire. A more expensive but very efficient solution is to use an infra-red lamp which will not disturb them, and which can be used much further from the kittens and therefore will not get in your way when attending to them.

In an emergency an ordinary hot water bottle may save a kitten's life. Wrap it up in a towel to diffuse the heat a little and make sure that it does not go cold or you will chill the kittens instead of warming them. If you have not got a hot water bottle a plastic bottle will make a good stop gap. Even simpler, if you have the means, is to raise the temperature of the whole room where the kittens are, although your family may find it unbearably hot.

Next to warmth, the kittens will need rest. They should not be disturbed unnecessarily and to prevent them disturbing each other you may find it useful to nestle each in a separate plastic box (without a lid of course) for although they normally snuggle together to keep warm each one, as it wakes, is likely to rouse the rest and none of them will get enough sleep. A loudly ticking clock (an alarm clock *with the bell turned off* is ideal) placed near them seems to give them a sense of security, perhaps because it reminds them of the beating of their mother's heart. Several layers of paper tissues will make comfortable bedding and are easily changed each day.

Ordinary cow's milk is no good for feeding kittens. Cat's milk has a much higher protein content and even the foods made for babies and puppies are not really suitable. Unsweetened evaporated milk (*not* condensed milk) is the simplest solution, but all cat breeders have their own formulae. One that has proved successful can be made up from: 2 tablespoons of condensed milk; 2 tablespoons of boiled water; $\frac{1}{4}$ teaspoon of corn syrup or glucose; $\frac{1}{4}$ teaspoon of concentrated beef extract.

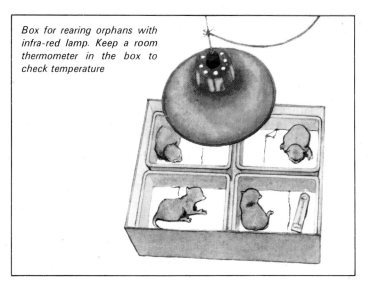

Box for rearing orphans with infra-red lamp. Keep a room thermometer in the box to check temperature

If you are lucky your local pet shop may stock a ready-made product specially formulated for kittens or your vet may be able to put you in touch with a source and you will have to resort to alternatives only in an emergency. If you have to take over the rearing of kittens straight from birth without their being fed at all by their mother ask your vet for help because they will be at greater risk — the first feeds given by the mother are full of antibodies which give immunity against the common cat diseases.

There are even more theories about feeding kittens than there are about feeding human babies. One and a half teaspoons of feed every four hours should be about right to begin with but if the formula is not rich enough they may need more. Gradually increase the amount as they grow. Be patient, some kittens will wolf it all down in a few minutes (and once they get to that stage probably splash it about so that they don't get enough) but others will take their time. Weigh each kitten each day and keep a record. If there is not a steady increase in weight there is something wrong. If a kitten cries for more food let him have it.

If your pet shop has a feeding bottle designed for kittens that will be the best way of giving them their milk. A doll's bottle, if it has a real working teat, will make a good substitute. You may prefer to use a dropper of the kind used for eye drops — or in times past for filling fountain pens. Be careful not to squeeze the rubber bulb and force the milk into the kitten's mouth, leave it to suck it out. If you force in too much milk you may choke the kitten or cause it to develop pneumonia — which claims many artificially raised kittens when they are only a few days old. As a very temporary measure, a twist of clean handkerchief soaked in milk can be given to a kitten to suck — but it must not be impregnated with washing powder residue or starch.

Don't try to feed a kitten in its box. Sit down with a coarse towel on your lap — to keep you clean and to give the kitten something to grip. Support the kitten against your palm holding its head gently between your thumb and index finger and offer the bottle or dropper with the other hand. The milk should be about 100°F (38°C). If the kitten isn't interested try a spot of milk formula on its nose to get it going or very gently squeeze a drop from the nipple while pushing it gently in and out of the kitten's mouth. If it gulps down too much and chokes then quickly raise its backside in the air to bring up any that went down the wrong way.

You should wind a kitten, just as you would a human baby, but instead of patting it over your shoulder rub its tummy to expel the air. Stroking it from head to tail with a corner of the towel will simulate the coarse action of its mother's tongue and a gentle massage under the tail with a cloth dipped in lukewarm water will stimulate it to evacuate. Its faeces should be neither runny nor too firm. If it has loose motions reduce the syrup or other liquids in the formula. You should also bathe the eyes each day with a swab soaked in saline solution, boracic acid solution or mineral oil. Wean orphans on to lapping liquids and eating solid food in the same way as with other kittens.

A cat mother will usually train her offspring not to soil the nest and to use a toilet tray as soon as they are physically capable of getting to it. If

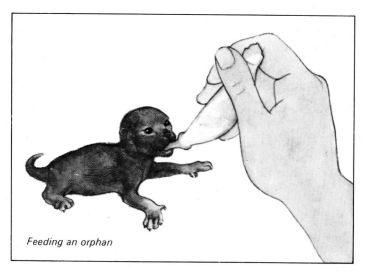
Feeding an orphan

you rear them yourself you will have to place them in the tray and encourage them to urinate or defecate by massaging them. In practice this causes fewer problems than you might imagine. Naturally little kittens will occasionally be too far from the tray to reach it in time to meet their needs, or the excitement of a game may make them forget themselves. A little tolerance may be necessary.

Start all their training as early as you can. Discourage them from playing with electric wiring, encourage them to use a scratching post, and, perhaps most importantly, get them used to being with people and groomed and handled by them. However, do not let young children play with very young kittens as accidents may happen.

If an isolated kitten gets an attack of diarrhoea there is no need to panic. It has probably just eaten something it should not have. Keep it off food for 12 hours and it will probably clear up — if you have one, give it a charcoal tablet. If the whole litter has the runs you may have made a change in the food formula, or served it too cold from the refrigerator. Perhaps the serving dish was not properly washed or the food left out too long. Try to work out the cause and try a starvation treatment. If the diarrhoea persists take a sample to the vet.

Your vet will also want a sample of motion if you think the kitten has worms. Some breeders will automatically worm all kittens to make sure that they are clear of them. Follow your vet's advice on the type of pills to use for the treatment has to be closely matched to the kitten's age and development.

Leaving mother
By eight or nine weeks old the kittens will have become very independent

and mother will probably be getting a little bored with them and their distracting games just when she feels like a nap. Nevertheless do not take all the kittens from her in one go. Some mothers part from their family without any fuss but others may go on searching for a missing kitten in a state of panic until they accept that it just is no longer there. Perhaps it is easier for the cat to see the new owners with the kitten so that she is reassured that it is in good hands, perhaps it is best that she does not actually see it being taken away. It depends upon the character of the cat and only experience can tell you what to do in an individual case.

After carefully rearing a litter you will want to make sure that the kittens go to good homes where they will be well looked after. If the potential new owners really want a kitten they will not mind in the least if you ask them lots of questions to establish that they are not taking their responsibilities lightly. If you have any doubts about them turn them down. Some people who have no wish to make money out of their kittens nevertheless insist on being paid for them just to make sure that the new people are serious. Pass on all the information you can about how you have been rearing a kitten, together with any pedigree registration and vaccination certificates and the name of your vet. Make sure they are aware of the need for further vaccinations and have the things they will need to make the kitten comfortable in its new home.

SHOWS AND SHOWING

Cat shows are held all over the world. They are very carefully run to strict standards laid down by the cat clubs and societies which organize them, but their regulations are by no means identical. The breeds which are recognized, the classes which may be entered and the methods of judging all vary according to the regulations under which they are run. In Britain there is a single body, the Governing Council of the Cat Fancy (GCCF), to which all lesser organizations seek affiliation. Its decisions are accepted throughout Britain and are followed by many of the clubs in the Commonwealth. In Canada and the United States there is no single such organization but a number of cat associations each of which issue their own set of breed Standards.

Different geography dictates a different pattern of shows in different places. In Britain, where few exhibitors travel very long distances to attend, shows last one day only but in the United States they are usually two-day affairs, held at the weekend if possible. On the European Continent some shows spread over three days, although the judging is completed on the first day if it can be.

In Britain, cats may not be exhibited at two shows within 14 days. This is to prevent the spread of any possible infection and it has the effect that shows are arranged, whenever practicable, with an interval of two weeks between each to enable cats to be entered in as many shows as their owners may wish.

Show classes
There is a wide variety of show classes for which prizes may be awarded. The most important in Britain are the Open classes for adults and kittens (which under the Governing Council of the Cat Fancy rules includes all cats up to the age of nine months) and there are a number of miscellaneous classes, including:

> *Senior:* for cats 2 years old or over.
> *Junior:* for cats under 2 years old.
> *Breeders:* for kittens bred by the exhibitor.
> *Notice:* for cats and kittens which have not won a First Prize under GCCF rules.
> *Limit:* for cats that have won not more than four First Prizes.
> *Special Limit:* for cats that have won not more than two First Prizes.
> *Debutante:* for cats and kittens that have never before been exhibited under GCCF rules.
> *Maiden:* for cats that have not won a First, Second or Third Prize under GCCF rules.

Novice Exhibitors: for cats whose owners have never won a money prize under GCCF rules even if the cat itself may be a prize winner.

Radius: for exhibitors living within a fixed distance of the exhibition hall.

Champions of Champions: for full Champions only.

Premier of Premiers: for full Premiers only.

Neuters have separate classes of their own and individual clubs may set up other special classes.

In North America the classes include the following for each Breed and colour:

Kittens: for cats over 4 months but under 8 months old.

Novices: for cats that have never won a first prize.

Open: for cats that have won a first prize.

Champion: for cats which have become Champions and hold the required certificate. A Champion is a cat holding four or more winner ribbons (six under the Cat Fanciers Association rules).

International Champion: for cats that are Champion in more than one country.

Grand Champions: for cats that are Grand Champions, qualification for which varies from association to association.

International Grand Champions: for cats that are International Grand Champions.

On the European Continent, kittens are defined as cats from 3 to 10 months old. There is a Grand International Champion class as in America, Champion and Open classes as in Britain and also two other kinds of competition:

Couples: for two cats of the same variety.

Breeder: for cats bred by the same person.

Most classes have a separate competition for neutered cats.

You do not necessarily have to own a pedigree cat to compete at a show. Many have classes for household pets which are judged purely on beauty and disposition.

Judging

All the cat associations require their judges to be experienced with cats and to meet the qualifications they lay down. The way of assessing each cat varies from organization to organization. Under British GCCF rules there are strict allocations of points for different aspects of each breed which are laid down in the breed Standard. The American Cat Fancier Association also uses a point-scoring method but many other associations use an overall evaluation by the judge. There is another big difference in approach: at North American Shows and most Continental ones the cats are taken to the judges whereas in British shows the judges go round the pens and only for the final "Best in Show" judging are cats taken up to the platform. For this reason the GCCF does not allow the cages to be decorated or to display previous ribbons or rosettes whereas in other shows the owner will decorate the pen to show the cat off to its best advantage.

In Britain there are three categories of show: Championship shows, where Challenge Certificates are given to whole cats who win the adult open classes and are considered worthy by the officiating judges (Premier Certificates are the equivalent for neuters); Sanction shows, similar but where Challenge certificates are not awarded; and Exemption shows which have less stringent rules and are intended for beginners. If a cat is awarded Challenge certificates at three different shows under three different judges the owner can apply to the GCCF to have it recognized as a Champion. Some shows select Best in Show, the best adult, kitten and neuter being chosen from Long-hairs, Short-hairs and Siamese or other type. Others choose Best of Breed for each variety.

In North America, a cat winning in one class qualifies to go forward to be judged in the next until, eventually, a Best Cat is chosen, together with a Second Best and a Best Opposite Sex. Best of each variety will also be chosen and best neuters. Kitten classes do not go forward for judgement against others. The Cat Fanciers Association instead of Best Opposite Sex select Best Cat down to Fifth Best.

Continental practice is similar to that in Britain. The winner of an Open class is given a Certificat d'Aptitude au Championnat. Three such wins qualify to become a Champion and enter the class for Champions only where a winner is awarded a Certificat d'Aptitude de Beauté. Three wins at this level qualify to compete for a Certificat d'Aptitude au Grand Championnat International and three such wins will take a cat to the highest European award and entitle it to the title Grand Championnat International.

Entering a show
You will find a calendar of shows regularly announced in the publications *Fur and Feather* for Britain and *Cats Magazine* for the United States and Canada. Write to the organizer for entry forms, list of classes and show rules. Your cat must already be registered with the appropriate authority if you propose to enter one of the pedigree classes. You will have to pay an entry fee for each class you enter and should send this, together with the completed form, to the organizer.

If everything is in order you will then receive all the necessary documentation, including a vetting-in card and a numbered tally to tie around the cat's neck. Check that the number agrees with that on the vetting-in card. Make sure that you can arrange to arrive and leave at the correct times. If travel arrangements are difficult apply for permission to arrive late or leave early as necessary. At some shows it may even be possible to arrange to leave the cat at the show hall the night before.

On arrival at the show each exhibit is examined by a veterinarian. Any suggestion of disease may mean that entry will be refused and your fee forfeited because no risk of infection can be allowed when there are so many cats gathered in one place. The vetting-in card is designed to speed up examination. Once passed you may make your cat comfortable in the pen corresponding to the number on your tally disc which should be put on white ribbon or tape and tied round the cat's neck. Where judges visit the pens you should provide the cat with a white blanket and a litter tray (peat moss is usually provided in the hall at GCCF shows) and food and water dishes will be needed for the time when feeding is allowed. Some owners fasten clear plastic sheeting across the front of the pen to prevent any visitors touching the cat through the bars. Competitors will usually be asked to leave the hall or to watch from a gallery when judging is actually in progress.

Preparing a cat for a show
Not all cats have the temperament to put up with many hours confined to a show cage after the disruptions of a journey while hundreds of people stare at them and strangers handle and inspect them. A cat that is upset will not be feeling or looking at its best, it may even show symptoms similar to those of a developing illness and fail to pass the vetting-in. It is important therefore to ensure that the cat is used to travelling and it should also be accustomed to the restricted show pen by being placed in a cage about two feet square for a few minutes each day and then for gradually longer periods until it can accept confinement for a whole day without distress.

You want your cat to look in peak condition so a little more than its regular grooming is called for. A dry shampoo a few days before the show, either with a proprietary shampoo or fuller's earth for light-coloured cats and oven-warmed bran for dark ones, will improve the coat. Rub the powder or bran into the fur with the tips of the fingers, especially where it feels greasy, and brush it out with a soft brush. Powder should be used about three days before the show and bran about five so that you can be sure that it will all be brushed out. There must be none left in the coat when it comes to the judging.

You need a basket to transport the cat and will want to take a clean blanket, water dish, food bowl, brush and comb and litter tray, together with a cloth and disinfectant if you want to wipe out the pen before putting your cat in it. Pens are disinfected by the organizers but at shows it is worth taking every precaution against the risk of infection. For short-haired cats a piece of velvet will be useful to polish the coat after you have given the eyes and ears a last-minute clean and the fur a final brush and comb just before the judging. Make sure that you have everything you need, especially your tally disc and vetting-in card, before you leave home.

Wipe the cat's eyes, ears, mouth and paws with a mild disinfectant as soon as the show is over, and when you get home make sure it has its favourite meal as a reward for putting up with the gruelling day. If possible keep it away from your other cats, just in case it has picked up some infection, and change and wash yourself before handling any of them.

BREEDS AND PEDIGREES

There is an enormous variety of cats with an almost endless permutation of conformation, colour, pattern, and coat length but only a limited number of them are recognized by cat fanciers as distinct breeds. These are variations which follow a regular type, pattern and colour and which have shown that over successive generations they consistently produce kittens with the same characteristics when like is bred to like. There are also some recognized breeds where this is not possible: Tortoiseshells and Blue Cream mixtures do not produce fertile males and must be mated with other breeds; however, they do consistently produce female Tortoiseshells or Blue Creams among their litters if carefully matched.

Experimental breeding is taking place all the time to develop new types of cat and to establish them breeding to type. If this can be shown through four generations and there are no retrograde characteristics perpetuating deformity, bad health or any other weakness they may then be accepted as a breed which may compete in shows governed by the various registration organizations. Naturally there are breeds which some associations recognize and others do not and there may be considerable argument as to whether a new breed should be given recognition.

New colour variations or new types of cat which have not received recognition may still enter competitive shows. In Britain they would contest in the Any Other Variety class and in North America they would appear as Non-Championship Provisional breeds. Experimental breeds, such as the Foreign Blue (a selfcolour of Foreign type) or the White Russian, which are not yet recognized and for which no Standard description has been agreed, appear on the show bench in this way; they have not been included in this book and some of the breeds that are described also have to be entered in these classes and are not eligible to compete for Championship status. A breed recognized in Europe will not necessarily be accepted by the British GCCF, nor will a British breed always be recognized by the North American bodies, who in their turn differ both in the breeds they recognize and details of the Standards they lay down for those they do accept.

In recent years a great deal of research has been undertaken into the genetic make-up of cats and breeding today is carried out on a very scientific basis. The study of genetics is a complex one, and the would-be breeder of a new variety should consult the literature on the subject. In general, however, a cat's characteristics will depend on which of the dominant genes it inherits from its parents. A female has 19 pairs of identical chromosomes, a male 18 such pairs and another 2 which do not match. This accounts for the sex-linking of certain characteristics such as the colour red. Certain characteristics will be dominant if a kitten inherits conflicting genes from its parents: tabby is dominant over non-tabby; white is dominant over all colours; black is dominant over blue and chocolate; short hair is dominant over long; all-over colour (self-coat) is dominant over the limited colouring of the Siamese or Himalayan. Although one feature may be dominant the other, or recessive, characteristic will still be present in the kitten's genetic pattern and will influence its progeny. There are many apparent anomalies: a mating, for instance, between a Blue Point and a Chocolate Point Siamese produces kittens of neither type but a litter which are all Seals! The Seal, which is actually the Siamese equivalent of Black, is carried by both parents for Blue and Chocolate are also modifications of Black. However, the next generation from these Seal kittens would produce Seals, Blues, Chocolates *and* Lilacs.

To predict what the results of a mating will be it is necessary to know the genealogy of the cat. Every cat has a pedigree but not many people control the matings of mongrel cats and even fewer attempt to keep a record of their pedigree. Although a pedigree is not synonymous with a recognized breed, in practice it is the established breeds of cats that are recorded and registered and for whom the pedigree is known. If you have your kittens neutered, a pedigree may only be of academic interest to you. If you are going to allow your cat to mate it is vitally important in helping to ensure fine and healthy kittens since it is not only the look of the cat but its health record which you have if you know or can find out as much as possible about the forebears. In this way the perpetuation of hereditary diseases and faults can be avoided and the overall quality of all cats improved.

THE SIAMESE CAT ASSOCIATION
PEDIGREE FORM

Name of Cat SAPA INSA

G.C.C.F. Registration Number

No. of Breed 24 C   **Colour** LILAC POINT   **Sex** MALE   **Date of Birth** 22 10 69

Owner MR LAWRENCE EASDEN   **Breeder** MR D SAM

Parents	Grand-Parents	Great Grand-Parents	Great Great Grand-Parents	
Sire IYANN RAJAH	**Sire** CHINKI RITZI	**Sire** MILORI BANZI 24	**Sire** CH BLUEHAYES FOXY	24
	89729 24		**Dam** CH MILORI LILI	24
		Dam CHINKI PETULA 24	**Sire** CH KILLDOWN SULTAN	24
			Dam CHINKI JUNITA	24
144512 24	**Dam** TAILONG FLORA	**Sire** CHAMPION TAILONG LUKI-LOOKI 24	**Sire** KERMA DEVI	24
	120870 24		**Dam** TAILONG PATCHULLI	24
		Dam CHAMPION ROSEWAY CINDERELLA 24A	**Sire** TORAPO	24
			Dam TRUBIA PENNY	24 A
Dam INCA ZAMESES	**Sire** ZAMESES 24	**Sire** SELBORNE PRAIRIE WOLF	**Sire** CH BLUE HAYES FOXY	
			Dam SELBORNE GEMINI	
		Dam CHAMPION TRAHA PACO ALLERGANDO	**Sire** BROWNDREYS CHUAN	24A
			Dam PRAHA SPICCATO	24A
17715 24	**Dam** TRUDENE FRANCOIS	**Sire** KATAQA BABA	**Sire** SHARKPEN BOBULIAK	
	17714 24B		**Dam** CALOWAY TUTTI	
		Dam FRANCESCA FROLIC	**Sire** SPUTLIGHT PRINCE	
			Dam FRANCESCA LOU	

PRIZES, etc.:

Signature

A pedigree form.

GUIDE TO CAT BREEDS

HAIRLESS CATS

All the cats which in the past were described as "hairless" actually had at least a downy covering. Occasionally a kitten of normal stock has the misfortune to be born bald and their unusual appearance has attracted the attention of experimental breeders. In France, for instance, a pair of Siamese carrying the recessive gene for baldness regularly produced hairless offspring which when mated together were found to breed true. The mutation has also been fixed in Canada by the breeders of the Sphynx. No hairless breed has been recognized by the GCCF and although the Sphynx has been recognized by the Canadian Cat Association, the Crown Cat Fanciers Association and the Cat Fanciers Association, the latter withdrew their provisional recognition in 1971.

MEXICAN HAIRLESS CAT

This breed is believed to be extinct. It is supposed to have been an Aztec breed and a pair owned by a Mr Shinick of New Mexico, which he had obtained from Mexican Indians at the beginning of this century, were said to be the last. The male was killed by a dog when still young and the pair never bred. They had long bodies, long tails and wedge-shaped heads with big ears. Their eyes were amber. They had long whiskers and in winter grew short fur along the back and tail which they shed as summer approached.

SPHYNX

The Sphynx, or Canadian Hairless as it is sometimes called, is very like the descriptions of the Mexican Hairless Cats but it has no whiskers and does not grow the winter ridge of fur. The breed has been developed from a hairless male born to a black-and-white house cat in Ontario in 1966. The longish body should be fine-boned but well-muscled with a long tail and a head that is neither round nor wedge-shaped but slopes outwards to the eyes and then forms a rectangular block from the eyes backwards. The golden-coloured eyes are set well back and slant slightly. The ears are set on a wide base and are large and very slightly rounded at the tips. The skin must be taut and without wrinkles except on the head. Kittens are covered with very fine short hair but as they become adult this is only noticeable on the points. A short pile which should "look like velvet and feel like moss" covers the face, growing longer on the back of the ears and heavy around the nose and the sides of the mouth. The paws and legs up to the wrist and ankle are covered in down and the back has microscopically fine hair like that on the mask. The last inch of the tail is covered in fine flat-lying hair. In males, the testicles are covered with a thick coat of hair which is longer than that anywhere else on the body. Sphynx cats may be any colour but solid-colour cats should be evenly coloured on the back and outer parts and blend into a lighter colour on the stomach and inside legs. A pink locket is acceptable around the neck but the only permitted white spots are around the nipples and the navel. The markings of parti-coloured cats should be arranged symmetrically.

The shortish nose and the set of the eyes, especially when combined with the bow-leggedness which appears in kittens, give a frontal look rather like that of a Boston Terrier.

When Sphynx cats appear at shows they attract a great deal of attention but feelings for and against such extreme examples of breed creation often run very high.

SPHYNX

SHORT-HAIRED CATS

Until the end of the 16th-century only short-haired cats seem to have been known in Europe. It is generally supposed that their basic coat pattern was usually tabby and that they looked rather like the European Wild Cat, for a tabby marking lurks in the background of all the breeds of European origin. However, grey cats appear in 16th-century Dutch pictures and Edward Topsell, presumably basing his observations on English cats, wrote at the beginning of the 17th century that "cats are of divers colours, but for the most part griseld, like to congealed ise." John Aubrey, the 17th-century English antiquarian, described how Archbishop Laud "was presented with some Cyprus-catts, *i.e.* our Tabby-catts, which were sold, at first for 5 pounds a piece: this was about 1637, or 1638." They were apparently a recent introduction and according to Aubrey "the common English Catt, was white with some blewish piedness." America's first domestic cats were taken across the Atlantic by European immigrants and they too were short-haired cats, like their parent stock.

Since the first cat show was held in England and it was in Britain that cat breeding was first taken seriously, the European type is usually known as the British Short-hair whilst cats with body conformation like the cats of the East are known as Foreign Short-hairs.

The British Short-hair is a sturdy strong-boned cat with a thick body set on short, well-proportioned legs. It is of medium length with a full chest. The shortish tail is thick at the base and tapers slightly to the tip. Front and back legs are of equal length with the feet neat and well rounded. The head is almost apple-shaped with the top of the skull rounded, well-developed cheeks and a short broad nose. The ears are small and slightly rounded and the eyes big, round and full of expression. The coat should be short and fine without harshness or woolliness.

Faults to look out for include ears that are too large, pointed or pricked, over-long nose, deepset or small eyes, a narrow face, legginess, or an open coat.

In the centuries since they were first taken to the New World, the North American domestic cat has developed slightly different characteristics from the British type and is recognized as the American Short-hair, or Domestic Short-hair as it is also called, with its own colour varieties and set of Standards (see page 97).

The Exotic Short-hair (see page 132) is a more recent American type which also receives recognition in the American Fancy, forming a link between the Long and Short-haired classes. It is not part of the Foreign type group of cats which have similar Standards throughout the world.

TABBY CATS

The name Tabby for the familiar striped or blotched pattern of so many of our domestic cats is probably derived from its similarity to a kind of watered silk or taffeta which was originally made at Attibiya, a district in Baghdad, and was also known as tabby. The old English name of "Cyprus cat", still used in some parts of East Anglia, also suggests some link through the eastern Mediterranean on the trade route which would have brought the silk to the West.

The Tabby's other name of Tiger Cat suggests the once commonly seen form of regular stripes, a pattern which is known to breeders as the Mackerel Tabby. Special classes are held for this type in the United States. The Standard Tabby pattern for the pedigree cat is carefully laid down and is certainly not possessed by all the non-pedigree domestic pets which are commonly called tabbies. The markings should always be strongly contrasted and free from brindling, whatever the colour variety of the cat.

In the Standard Tabby three dark stripes run down the spine, a butterfly pattern can be seen across the shoulders, an "oyster"-shaped whorl appears on the flanks, and on the chest there are two unbroken narrow lines known as the "mayoral chains." Legs and tail are regularly ringed and the face carries delicate pencilling running down to the base of the nose while the cheeks are crossed by two or three distinct swirls. A well-marked Tabby will usually also have a clearly defined pair of "spectacles" around the eyes and on the forehead the "M" mark which legend says commemorates the prophet Mohammed.

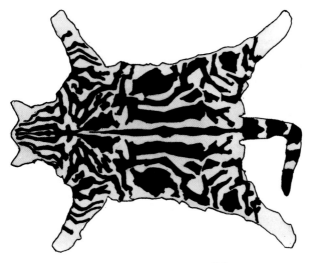

STANDARD TABBY PATTERN

The Mackerel Tabby should have equally distinct markings in the form of dense narrow rings which run around the body, legs and tail. The stripes are sometimes broken, but should not break up into spots, and clear rings running from the spine to the ground are preferred. Although this was the original form of the tabby pattern, examples with clear, narrow, closely-spaced stripes and general type of show standard are comparatively rare and they have become unusual on the show bench in Britain. The classic blotched tabby pattern is a mutation of the striped Tabby which developed in Europe and was already common by the middle of the 17th century. There is no evolutionary precedent for this pattern in wild cats but it appears to be successful in all kinds of environment and had reached India by the mid-19th century; however, the striped cat still seems to be in the majority in India and the blotched pattern is not yet well-established in the East. There is no indication that breeders or owners prefer blotched Tabbies so it is difficult to understand why this mutation should have proved so persistent.

It is rare for variants other than forms of the blotched and striped patterns to occur naturally, although the ticked or agouti coat of the Abyssinian cat is genetically a form of Tabby. However, a careful selection of Tabbies with variant markings has led to the development of the Egyptian Mau and the Spotted Cat. The Tabby marking persists in many other created breeds and shows in their first kitten coats, while parts of the Tabby marking have been retained in breeds such as the Lynx or Tabby Point Siamese.

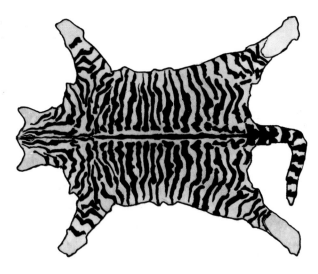

MACKEREL TABBY PATTERN

BROWN TABBY SHORT-HAIR

Although this is one of the oldest established breeds it is comparatively rare as a pedigree cat. This may be partly because non-pedigree cats of Brown Tabby type can be seen so frequently, and in choosing a pedigree pet owners look for something more unusual, but it is probably even more due to the difficulty of producing a cat of really good type and colour.

Brown Tabby to Brown Tabby matings which are continued through several generations seem to lead to a falling off in type, so that skilful breeding management is required. Distinct markings without any brindling or smudging are difficult to achieve and white patches, especially on the chin and lip can be persistent. The Brown Tabby should conform to the general standard for Short-hairs. The markings, which may follow the blotched or mackerel pattern, should be very dense and black, not mixed with the ground colour and quite distinct from it. The ground colour should be a rich sable or brown and uniform throughout with no white spots or markings anywhere. The eyes should be orange, hazel, deep yellow or green.

RED TABBY SHORT-HAIR

Although the Red Tabby has often been described as a ginger or marmalade cat, the pedigree cat of show standard will be neither ginger nor sandy in colour but a rich deep orange-red with the markings in an even darker red.

BROWN TABBY SHORT-HAIR

Although the colour is not uncommon among non-pedigrees cats it is difficult to find clearly defined markings which do not mix with the ground colour to give a blurred effect of shading rather than distinct bars. Pedigree kittens born with quite clear markings may lose them during the first few weeks of life but they should regain their colour and definition as they get older.

It was once believed that only male Red Tabbies were produced and that they were sterile. Both beliefs are fallacies. Matings with a black female will produce black males and tortoiseshell females. Matings with tortoise-shells (who carry the red gene) may produce black or red males and red or tortoiseshell females. A black male can also be mated with a tortoiseshell to produce red or black males and tortoiseshell or black females. The Red Tabby should conform to the general Standard for Short-hairs. The markings of the coat should be dark red and very dense and must be quite distinct from the ground colour. Both ground colour and markings should be as rich as possible. The eyes should be hazel or orange.

SILVER TABBY SHORT-HAIR

As with all Tabbies, the markings, whether mackerel or marbled, should be distinct and well contrasted. The ground colour should be a pure clear silver of uniform hue throughout and without any trace of white on either body or tail. The markings should be a dense black. The eyes should be well-opened, round and green or hazel in colour. Kittens which are clearly marked at birth frequently become greyish as their fur grows but this resolves into a good pattern when they are about 15 weeks old.

French breeders, and some in Britain, have introduced a short-haired Black at every fourth generation as a means of maintaining good type and dense markings.

This extremely beautiful cat is also one of the most affectionate. They are gentle and shy but make sturdy and hardy pets which seem to maintain their fine appearance with very little grooming.

SPOTTED CAT

Spotted cats were at one time common and were exhibited at the earliest cat shows, when they were frequently treated as a variety of the Tabby. But they did not reappear on the show bench until the 1960s and were again recognized as a separate variety in Britain with their own Standard in 1966. Spotted cats appear quite frequently in Greece and other parts of the Mediterranean but the Spotted Cat of British type is still comparatively rare. The British Standard awards 75 points to the pattern alone which should be distinct but does not have to consist entirely of circular spots. They may be round, oblong or rosette shaped but they should not give the appearance of broken stripes. Stripes and bars are definite faults except when they appear on the head which will usually have tabby-like markings.

RED TABBY SHORT-HAIR

SILVER TABBY SHORT-HAIR

Spotted cats may be any colour, provided that there is a good contrast between the ground colour and the spots and that the eyes conform with the Standards laid down for the main coat colour in British Short-hairs. In all other respects, too, the cat should conform to the requirements for British type. So many of the cat's wild relations have a spotted coat that it is surprising that this pattern is not seen more often in domestic cats.

MANX

The tailless Manx has been known for centuries and there are many legends to account for its origin and its arrival on the Isle of Man. One far-fetched story tells how Phoenician sailors brought it back from a voyage to Japan. Another, how a female cat bit off her kittens' tails to prevent them being slaughtered so that Manx warriors could wear their bushy tails as helmet plumes. Simplest of all is the explanation that the Manx was late in reaching Noah's ark and the impatient patriarch, eager to set sail as the waters rose, slammed the door shut and cut off her tail.

In fact tailless cats occur in many parts of the world. Charles Darwin reported them throughout the Malayan region. There are tailless cats in China, in Russia – especially the Crimea – and in many other places. Perhaps the Phoenician story has a grain of truth in that they may have spread through ships trading out of the Black Sea. Presumably it was the restricted breeding pattern imposed by island conditions which led to the development of a particular strain upon the Isle of Man, not that the Manx is a breed in the sense that it will always breed true. Manx parents will often produce a litter which includes kittens with tails and "stumpies" – kittens with an abbreviated tail. Similarly, fully tailed cats may carry the mutant gene for taillessness and produce Manx-like kittens in their litters.

A Manx or rumpy, as they are sometimes called, is more than just a tailless cat. It has a special coat which is double, soft and open, like that of a rabbit, with a short thick undercoat. The main characteristics are as for British Short-hairs but the head is larger, without approaching the snubby Persian type, with a longish nose but chubby cheeks which maintain its roundness. The ears are set well apart and are wide at the base tapering to a point. The back is relatively short and the hindquarters are very high with a deep flank. This helps to give the Manx a characteristic bobbing gait. The long hind legs also give it a powerful spring and help to make it a faster cat than most. The taillessness must be complete with no vestige of a tail. It should be possible to feel a hollow at the end of the backbone. The rump should be well rounded: the British Standard says "as round as an orange." Some Manx, although completely tailless, have a small tuft of fur on the rump. This is acceptable if it contains no cartilage or bone.

Manx may be any colour and pattern: bi-colour, tabby, tortoiseshell or self-colour but the colour of the eyes must agree with the coat as for similarly coloured British Short-hairs. In judging, eye colour, coat colour and pattern are only considered if more important characteristics are equal.

SPOTTED SHORT-HAIR

MANX

The lack of tail does not appear to affect the Manx's sense of balance but it has been observed that they are rarely such good climbers as other cats and will ignore bird's nests. Instead they are usually good rodent hunters and often make fine fishermen.

The Manx has a very definite personality of its own and can make a delightful pet. But the mutation which makes it tailless affects the entire vertebral column: although the reduction in the length and number of vertebrae is usually concentrated at the rear, vertebrae can be missing from other regions causing other malformations. The greater the malformation the higher the infant mortality rate and Manx bred to Manx through several successive generations may produce dead kittens. A malfunction of the sphincter muscles of the anus is one of the abnormalities which is sometimes associated with the malformation of the Manx. A "stumpy", whatever the length of tail, will be assured of a normal life.

CREAM SHORT-HAIR

Cream Short-hairs are difficult to breed and are still comparatively rare. Natural Creams occasionally occur but they are usually striped or barred, and it is only since World War II that the pale Creams, now much admired, have replaced the over-"hot" fawn or orangey-coloured cat which is the link between this and the Red Tabby. The Cream is presumably a development of the Red Tabby since, genetically, cream is a dilute of red, although no short-haired British Red Self breed exists as the tabby markings in the hotter colour remain predominant.

The Cream follows the Standard set for British Short-Hair type and the coat should be a rich cream free from barring and with no sign of white anywhere. The eyes could be deep copper or orange. Prior to 1967, the British Standard permitted hazel eyes but they are not now allowed.

Kittens with barred markings often lose them as they grow older but the pattern is so strong that it can reappear during unusually hot or cold weather.

BLUE-EYED WHITE SHORT-HAIR

White short-haired cats should conform to the overall requirements for the British type with a broad head, well-formed cheeks, small, slightly rounded ears and a short nose and face, a sturdy body, thick-rooted tail and neat well-rounded feet. The close, fine coat should be pure white with no trace of creaminess and no coloured hairs. The eyes should be a deep sapphire blue.

In Britain a white cat used to be thought unlucky, although in the United States and several continental countries it was considered to be a good omen. Everywhere today white cats seem to be popular, but they are not easy to find. They do not often occur under natural breeding conditions, perhaps because a white cat would be very noticeable and therefore more

CREAM SHORT-HAIR

BLUE-EYED WHITE SHORT-HAIR

vulnerable in the wild, and perhaps also because white cats with blue eyes are almost without exception deaf, which would also operate against it in natural selection.

If a Blue-eyed White kitten has a tiny patch of dark hair — no more than a smudge — on the head between the ears this is an indication that it genetically carries black or blue and that its hearing will be sound. In most cases the dark hair will disappear as the kitten grows.

ORANGE-EYED WHITE SHORT-HAIR

It is impossible to tell at birth which of the varieties a white kitten will grow up to be as all kittens start life with blue eyes — the deeper the blue the more likely they are to stay that colour. If they become orange you need not worry about the deafness problem. Orange-eyed White should be identical to their Blue-eyed relatives except for the eye colour which should be a rich golden orange or copper. (Illustrated on page 89).

ODD-EYED WHITE SHORT-HAIR

A third variety of White Short-hair has one blue eye and one orange eye. In every other respect they should, like the other eye colours, conform to the requirements for a British Short-hair and have pure white fur untinged with yellow. They are sometimes said to be deaf on the side of the blue eye but this is not necessarily so. Odd-eyed Whites are born in both Blue-eyed and Orange-eyed litters and are used in breeding both these varieties. (Illustrated on page 89).

BLACK SHORT-HAIR

Black cats, in particular, have been associated with witchcraft and were once even thought to be a form taken by the devil. Since the long-haired cat was unknown in Europe in the Middle Ages, it is the short-haired Black that suffered from the superstition of the times. By contrast many people, particularly in Britain, have in recent times considered a black cat particularly lucky, and this has made them very popular. But, although there are many black cats about, there are relatively few which would conform to the Standards laid down for the official short-haired breed evolved by many years of careful breeding. Black Short-hairs should have the proper British Short-hair type and their large, well-opened eyes should be a deep orange or copper: most of the cats you see about are too sleek in the body and have green eyes. The coat must also be a true jet black to the roots with no trace of a white hair anywhere and no sign of the brownish tinge known as "rustiness." Many kittens carry faint tabby stripes when young and most show a certain degree of rustiness, which may not grow out until they are fully adult. Any black cat which spends a great deal of time in the

BLACK SHORT-HAIR

sun will also develop a rusty tinge, and one that enjoys sunbathing is best kept away from the show bench during the summer months. Greasiness can also cause discolouration and to keep the coat in show condition will demand constant attention. Handgrooming with a piece of chamois leather will give an extra lustre to the close-set fur.

BRITISH BLUE

Blue, in cat terminology, does not mean a bright sky blue but a bluish grey. The colouring is a dilute form of black and according to the British Standard may range from light to medium blue but it must be "very level in colour" with no tabby markings, shading or white hairs anywhere. This is much lighter than the dark slate colour which was favoured in the past and has now been bred out of show cats.

The British Blue should be of British Short-hair type but, although not mentioned in the Standard, the short fine coat is more plush-like than in some of the other varieties. The broad head with well-developed cheeks and short nose probably comes closer to the British Standard than in most other short-hair cats. The eyes should be large and full and a rich copper, orange or yellow colour.

This breed has a reputation for gentleness and placidity; they are also extremely intelligent.

In America the Cat Fanciers Association list an Exotic Short-hair (Blue) which is, in effect, the same cat as the British Blue.

The mating of a British Blue male to a Cream female can produce Cream males and Blue Cream females; to a Blue Cream female the litter may include Blue and Cream males, and Blue and Blue Cream females. A British Blue female mated to a Cream male may have Blue-Cream females and Blue males.

CHARTREUX

A French breed, said to have been taken to France from South Africa by Carthusian monks, which is now almost identical to the British Blue although the French Standard specifies a coat of any shade of grey or greyish blue. This used to be a more massive cat than the British breed but its sturdy, well-muscled look, rounded head, strong jaws and well-developed cheeks make up a cat which judges agree to be the same as the modern British Blue. The continental cat also has the same gentle and intelligent character and is reputed to be a fine mouser.

MALTESE

The short-haired Blue cats exhibited in the early North American shows were often shown under the name Maltese, and Maltese has from time to time been used elsewhere to signify a blue colouration. These cats were either light or dark blue and some had white spots on the chest. There also seems to have been considerable variation in type, some having large heads, some small, some cobby bodies, some not. The name is no longer used for any recognized breed but the old Maltese cats played an important role in the development of the present-day short-haired Blue.

BLUE CREAM SHORT-HAIR

This difficult-to-breed variety is one of the rarest in Britain and was not recognized by the GCCF until 1956. It is an all female variety. Cream, a dilute of red, is a sex-linked factor. They can be produced from Blue and Cream matings and in tortoiseshell litters if both parents carry blue.

The Blue Cream's coat should be short and fine in texture with the colours "softly mingled, not patched," according to the British Standard. A cream blaze or streak on the forehead is favoured by many breeders and gives the cat a very distinguished look when set against a well-mingled face. The eyes should be copper, orange or yellow but must not be green. In all other respects the Blue Cream conforms to the British Short-hair type. They are almost invariably cats of great charm with very pleasant personalities.

In North America the Blue Cream Short-hairs of both Domestic and

BRITISH BLUE

BLUE CREAM SHORT-HAIR

Exotic type are required to have a clearly patched, instead of a mingled, coat. Breeders on either side of the Atlantic are working to exactly opposite goals. (See pages 97 and 132).

SMOKE SHORT-HAIR

No Smoke variety of British type is recognized as a breed but there are both Black Smoke and Blue Smoke cats among the American Short-hair breeds (see page 97), and a provisional standard for a British type Smoke Short-hair exists on the European continent.

BI-COLOURED SHORT-HAIR

Bi-coloured Cats, or Parti-coloured Cats as they are also known in the United States, are cats of two distinctly different colours. The Black-and-White, once known as the Magpie, has long been admired and an old Standard required it to have very exact markings on different parts. Later requirements, limiting the colours to black and white, blue and white, orange and white and cream and white, demanded that the coat be patterned like that of a Dutch rabbit. The ears and mask were to be coloured and the colour began again behind the shoulders and swept down the body tail and hind legs leaving the hind feet, neck, forelegs and feet, chin and lips white. A white blaze up the centre of the face and over the head was to divide the face exactly in half continuing white on the back of the skull.

These very strict requirements were so difficult to meet that in 1971 the British Standard was revised to permit "any solid colour and white; the patches of colour to be clear and evenly distributed. Not more than two-thirds of the cat's coat to be coloured and not more than one-half to be white. Face to be patched with colour, and white blaze desirable." The cat should be of the usual British type but the Standard elaborates, requiring its body to be "hard and muscular, giving a general appearance of activity" and "cobby, with short straight legs." The head has to be "round and broad, width between ears, which should be small and well placed. Short nose, full cheeks, wide muzzle and firm chin (level bite)."

The eyes should be large, round and set well apart. They must be deep orange, yellow or copper and any trace of green is considered a fault. Other faults are tabby markings or brindling in the coat or too long a tail, which should be short and thick.

TORTOISESHELL SHORT-HAIR

These black-and-red cats, which have been variously known in North America as Calimanco Cats and Clouded Tigers as well as by their usual name, are difficult to breed for, however it is mated, there is no guarantee

BI-COLOURED SHORT-HAIR

TORTOISESHELL SHORT-HAIR

that a single one of a Tortoiseshell cat's litter will turn out like its mother. Males are seldom born and are almost invariably sterile (although there is a record of two males which sired litters at the beginning of this century) so like-to-like breeding is not possible. Mating may be with a black or cream male but tabbies have to be avoided for their coat pattern would prove dominant and be very difficult to eradicate in future generations. A finely marked Tortoiseshell is a very beautiful cat and however their markings are placed they give their appearance great character. Kittens, especially those which will be well marked when adult, are usually very dark when born and the coloured patching appears as the fur grows. There should only be three colours in the coat: black, light red and dark red, and the British Standard requires that the colours be equally balanced and each as brilliant as possible. There should be no trace of white anywhere, and no sign of tabby markings or brindling. The patches of colour should be clear and defined with no blurring and legs, feet, tail and ears should be as well patched as the body and head. A red blaze running down the forehead to the nose is particularly desirable. The eyes should be orange, copper or hazel. In other respects this breed follows the standards for the British Short-hair.

TORTOISESHELL AND WHITE SHORT-HAIR (CALICO SHORT-HAIR)

In this breed the tri-colour patching of the Tortoiseshell is handsomely set off against white but to reach show standard the balance and arrangement of the colouring must be in accordance with the Standard and cats with a predominance of white fur would be faulted. The British Standard demands: "Black and red (dark and light) on white, equally balanced. Colours to be brilliant and absolutely free from brindling, or tabby markings. The tri-colour patchings should cover the top of the head, ears and cheeks, back and tail and part of flanks. Patches to be clear and defined. White blaze desirable."

The eyes should be orange, copper or hazel and in all structural points the cat should conform to the British Short-hair type.

Tortoiseshell and White colouring has had a wide distribution. Japanese sailors used to like to have one of these cats on their ships for they believed that they would bring them luck and keep away the evil spirits of the ocean which brought storm and shipwreck. They were known to Europeans and in America as Spanish Cats and the 18th-century French naturalist, Georges Buffon, believed they owed the beauty of their colouring to their supposed native Spanish climate.

TORTOISESHELL AND WHITE SHORT-HAIR

AMERICAN SHORT-HAIR (DOMESTIC SHORT-HAIR)

For a long time the American domestic cat, descended from the cats taken to North America by the early settlers, was unrecognized as a distinct breed for show purposes; but they now receive full recognition from the various cat associations and carry off top awards at many shows. Developed from the same basic stock as the common European moggy, the pedigree American Short-hair is very similar to the pedigree British Short-hair but there are distinct differences and many breeders would consider the Exotic Short-hair (see page 132) a closer match to the British type.

The American Short-hair is a well-built cat with a medium to large body set on sturdy, firm-boned legs of medium length. The firm, rounded paws should have heavy pads. The medium-length tail should be heavy at the root and although the vertebrae taper in the normal way it appears to come to an abrupt, blunt end. Very short or kinked tails would be faults in a show cat. The chest and shoulders are well developed and the medium-length neck should be of an even width and gently curved carrying a large, full-cheeked head only slightly longer than it is wide so that it has an oblong look. The nose is longer than in the British type but the muzzle is more square and the chin is firm and well-developed. The ears have slightly rounded tips and are set well apart but are not particularly wide at the base. The eyes are wide-set, large and round with a slight slant to the outer edge. The coat should be thick, short and even with a hard texture, not so plushy as the British cat, and it grows heavier and thicker during the colder months. It must not be long or fluffy.

Overall, as one Standard puts it, the effect should be that of "the trained athlete, with all muscles rippling easily beneath the skin, the flesh lean and hard, and with great latent power held in reserve." These cats have a reputation for easy jumping and the earlier history of the type has ensured that they are tough and hardy animals. They are affectionate and intelligent and make excellent pets.

American Short-hairs are now recognized in the following colour varieties, some of which do not exist in the British Short-hair: White (blue-eyed, copper-eyed and odd-eyed), Black, Blue, Red, Cream, Chinchilla (pure fur delicately tipped with black on the back, sides, head, ears and tail), Shaded Silver (Silver fur with shadings on the sides, face and tail giving a much darker effect than in the Chinchilla), Black Smoke (Black tipping to short white fur), Blue Smoke (Blue tipping to short white fur), Tortoiseshell, Calico (Tortoiseshell and White), Blue Cream (the two colours to be in clearly defined patches, not mingled as in the British Standard), Brown, Blue, Red, Silver and Cream Tabby (both striped and blotched patterns). Bi-colours are also bred.

AMERICAN WIRE-HAIR

In 1966 a chance mutation produced a farmyard kitten with very coarse and wiry fur and careful breeding is developing his progeny into a new breed which will have this medium-length coat of stiff hair which is wiry on the head, back, sides and hips and along the top of the tail, but becomes less coarse on the underside of the body and chin. The American Wire-hair Cat Society has proposed a Standard describing the breed as a "spontaneous mutation of the domestic cat. The only difference between the domestic and the wire-hair is the coat."

BOMBAY

A recently developed variety created in the United States from crossings between Burmese and American Short-hairs. It is a medium-sized but muscular cat with a rounded head with medium-sized ears that are slightly rounded at the tips. The Bombay's short coat is a lustrous black with an almost glass-like sheen. The eyes are yellow to deep copper.

AMERICAN SHORT-HAIR

AMERICAN WIRE-HAIR

SCOTTISH FOLD

Old natural histories often include reports of cats with drooping ears. It has been noted that wild animals almost invariably had pricked ears and only among long-domesticated species did they droop. In 1796 the *Universal Magazine of Knowledge and Pleasure* confidently recorded that "domestic cats have not such stiff ears as the wild, and at China, which is an empire very anciently policed, and where the climate is very mild, domestic cats may be seen with hanging ears. . . ." The idea of a drop-eared Chinese breed was a persistent one. A century later a sailor returned from China with a drop-eared cat which he claimed was one of a breed raised there for food. However, zoologists found no trace of any others until 1938 when a second cat was found and the characteristic proved to be a rare mutation which was then thought to be restricted to white long-haired cats.

The mutation reappeared in Scotland in 1961 and controlled breeding has produced a variety of short-haired cats with ears folded forward and downward. Similar mutations have also appeared in Germany and Belgium and several have been imported into the United States. No Standards have been accepted and although a kitten whose ears had not yet developed the distinctive droop won a prize at a British Show in 1971, the GCCF has not recognized the breed. There is considerable opposition to its development but in 1974 it was recognized for registration by the CFA.

SCOTTISH FOLD

FOREIGN SHORT-HAIRED CATS

The description "Foreign" has nothing to do with the country of origin of this group of cats, although some of their forebears may have come from overseas. They include types developed in Britain, North America and on the European Continent and there are cats from other territories which do not appear in the Foreign group.

In general they can be said to have slim bodies, long tails and slender legs giving a very elegant and sophisticated appearance. Their heads are wedge-shaped with large pricked ears and slanting eyes. While individual breeds differ, generally they do not like a solitary life and demand the attention of humans or the companionship of another cat. They tend to mature early and females may begin to call when only about six months old. Males are not quite so advanced but entire cats may be sexually mature earlier than other breeds.

Foreign type cats are easy to groom. A short-bristled brush followed by a rub with a chamois leather will give the coat a beautiful sleek look and handgrooming alone will give their coats a polished sheen.

Some Foreign cats, especially Siamese, Burmese and Russian Blues, are particularly susceptible to Feline Enteritis. It is vital that they are innoculated as early as possible.

ABYSSINIAN CAT

In 1868 a British military expedition returned from Abyssinia and with them apparently came a Mrs Barret-Lennard bearing a cat called Zulu which was reputed to be the first Abyssinian to reach Britain. A portrait published six years later shows a cat quite unlike the breed we know today and this version of the breed's origin can probably be discounted. Nevertheless, the breed was already being listed by 1882 and a photograph of 1903 shows a cat that is a fine example of the modern type. The Abyssinian also looks remarkably like the cat shown in ancient Egyptian art and has the agouti coat of the African Wild Cat which played a major role in the evolution of the domestic cat.

Some Abyssinian owners like to think of their cat as a direct descendant of the cats of the pharaohs but there is no evidence to support the idea. However, cats very similar to the Abyssinian type are born from time to time to ordinary tabbies and after carefully planned breeding from them they can eventually breed to type. The Abyssinian may be a reversion to the form of the ancient cat, but it is almost certainly also a new creation produced by the skill of British breeders.

Two Abyssinian cats were taken to America in 1909 but it was many years before the breed became popular in the United States. The number registered is now exceeded only by the Siamese and the Burmese and there are far more Abyssinians in America than there are in Britain.

The Abyssinian has a slender body and a long, tapering tail. Its legs are fairly slender and it has neat oval feet. Although it is more solidly built than the Siamese and Burmese it is of noticeably Foreign type. The British Standard demands that the head be "a medium wedge of heart-shaped proportions" while in America, where a slightly blunter muzzle is preferred, it is described in the Cat Fanciers Association Standard as "a modified wedge without flat planes; the brow, cheeks and profile lines all showing a gentle contour." The largish ears are sharp at the tip and broad at the base. The eyes are large and may be green, gold or hazel.

The Abyssinian's coat is its most important feature. Each hair has two or three distinct bands of black or dark brown on the ruddy brown ground, which account for the subtle overall coat colour. There should be no bars or other markings, although a dark line down the spine will not militate against an otherwise good show cat. The belly and the inside of the forelegs are a lighter shade which should harmonize with the main colour — orange-brown is preferable. The nose leather should be brick-red, outlined in black, and the paw pads should be black, as should the back of the hind legs. There should be no white markings on the body but a white chin, although undesirable, is permitted. Many cats have a cream or off-white area around the chin and lips and together with the light areas around the eyes, which are closely rimmed in black with black or brown markings on the forehead just above them, this gives a puma-like appearance which can be very attractive. If the tail is barred the tip should be dark brown or black. Some kittens show very heavy markings which fade as they get older. The agouti ticking does not usually show until the kitten is about two months old.

The Abyssinian is an affectionate and highly intelligent cat which is much in demand. They usually have smaller litters than other breeds, four kittens or fewer are common so that they may not be very easy to obtain. They enjoy a lot of attention but like to roam and may be unhappy if confined.

RED ABYSSINIAN

The Red Abyssinian has been recognized as a separate breed since 1963. It is the same as the Standard Abyssinian in every way except colour which should be a rich copper red with each hair doubly or trebly ticked with a darker colour. The belly and inside of the legs should be deep apricot. The tail tip is dark brown and this colour can extend in a line along the top of the tail or even along the spine. The nose leather is pink as are the pads which should be set in brown fur that extends up the back of the legs. The almond-shaped eyes may be green, yellow or hazel.

Cream Abyssinians have also been bred but they still await official recognition.

ABYSSINIAN (RUDDY ABYSSINIAN)

RED ABYSSINIAN

RUSSIAN BLUE

One name for the Russian Blue used to be the Archangel Cat and the first may have been brought from that Russian port by British sailors and merchants who were trading there in the time of Elizabeth I, but blue cats can appear as a natural mutation and have also been known as Maltese. Earlier this century, when the British name for the type was Foreign Blue an English breeder obtained two queens that actually came from Archangel. The first to appear in America was imported to Chicago around the turn of the century but the breed did not become established in the United States until after World War II. By then Scandinavian and British breeders had begun to introduce Siamese blood and in 1950 the Foreign Blue had a Standard which required an all-blue Siamese type cat. There has now been a return to the original type and both British and American Standards now require a cat with a long and graceful body, with medium-strong bone structure, which has a fairly long, tapering tail, long legs, small oval feet and a short wedge-shaped head with a flat, narrow skull and a straight forehead and nose which form an angle. The nose is shorter than in the Siamese. The eyes are almond-shaped and set rather wide apart. They should be vivid green when adult. The ears look large and pointed, wide at the base and set vertically to the head. A particular characteristic of the breed is the thinness of the skin of the ears which should be nearly transparent and there should be little furnishing inside the ear. The whisker pads are prominent.

The coat should be a clear blue colour and although some tabby marking may be evident in kittens, this should disappear as they grow older and there should be no shading. In Britain, a medium blue is preferred but the evenness of colour is more important than the shade. There should be a distinct silvery sheen which is produced by the double coat. The British Standard requires the fur to stand up "soft and silky like seal skin." It must be short, thick and very fine and silver tipping to each hair enhances the desired effect. This becomes particularly prominent in the winter, while strong summer sunshine may give the coat a brownish hue.

Russian Blues have a reputation for gentleness. They are sometimes very shy and usually have very quiet voices so that it may be difficult to know when a queen is on heat if you do not know the cat well. However, they become very attached to their owners so this is not likely to create problems. They seem to adapt well to life in apartments.

BROWN BURMESE

This breed, known in France as Zibelines, was first accepted for registration in America in 1936 but was not known in Europe until after World War II. The first American cat was imported from India and, despite the name, the connection with Burma is not established. In fact this cat was found to be a hybrid Siamese, the cross being a previously unidentified breed with a dark coat. It was mated to Siamese and when the hybrids among the

RUSSIAN BLUE

BROWN BURMESE

kittens were bred dark-coated Burmese were produced. The genes which produce the Burmese and Siamese colouring belong to the same series but the cats do not look alike. Despite earlier descriptions the Burmese is *not* a dark-coated Siamese, although at one time the demand for this beautiful cat led to so much cross-breeding with Siamese that many so-called Burmese were exactly that and, as a result, the Cat Fanciers Association withdrew recognition for a number of years. The British Standard makes the point quite clear: "The Burmese is an elegant Cat of a foreign type, which is positive and quite individual to the breed. Any suggestion of either Siamese type, or the cobbiness of a British cat, must be regarded as a fault.

"The body should be of medium length and size, feeling hard and muscular and heavier than its appearance indicates. The chest should be strong and rounded in profile, the back straight from shoulder to rump. Legs should be slender and in proportion to the body; hind legs slightly longer than the front: paws neat and oval in shape. The tail should be straight and of medium length, not heavy at base, and tapering only slightly to a rounded tip without bone defect.

"The head should be slightly rounded on top, with good breadth between the ears, having wide cheek bones and tapering to a short blunt wedge. The jaw should be wide at the hinge and the chin firm. A muzzle pinch is a bad fault. Ears should be medium in size, set well apart on the skull, broad at the base, with slightly rounded tips, the outer line of the ears continuing the upper part of the face. This may not be possible in mature males who develop a fullness of cheek. In profile the ears should be seen to have a slight forward tilt. There should be a distinct nose break, and in profile the chin should show a strong lower jaw. The eyes, which must be set well apart, should be large and lustrous, the top line of the eye showing a straight oriental slant towards the nose, the lower line being rounded." This Standard, introduced in 1974, and that introduced in the United States in 1959, demand a rather shorter, more compact cat, with a rounder head than that which was previously accepted. The American Standard also asks for round feet and round eyes. The eye colour in both territories should be yellow, the more intensely golden the better.

The coat should be short, fine and close-lying with a satin-like texture. The colour should be a rich warm seal-brown, shading almost imperceptibly to a slightly lighter shade on the underparts. The ears and mask may be slightly darker but there should be no other shading or markings, although faint tabby barrings in kittens and a few white hairs will be ignored by judges if the cat is otherwise excellent. Nose leather and foot pads should be brown. Kittens are often coffee coloured when young but they darken with age. However, a very dark colour, bordering on black, is incorrect. Burmese are intelligent and friendly cats, less vocal and not so highly strung as the Siamese.

BLUE BURMESE

BLUE BURMESE

The first recorded Burmese in which the appearance of a recessive gene
for blue produced a lighter-coloured kitten was a British-born cat bred
from an imported American father in 1955. Five years later sufficient
blue-to-blue matings had taken place and pure-bred kittens produced for
the GCCF to give the Blue Burmese breed status and several of the North
American registration bodies now recognize it as a distinct variety.

The British Standard requires the adult coat to be "a soft silver grey
only very slightly darker on the back and tail. There should be a distinct
silver sheen on rounded areas such as ears, face and feet." As this indicates,
the coat is warmer in tone with less blue than those of the Russian and
British Blues. The paw pads should be grey and the nose leather very dark
grey. In other respects the Blue follows the requirements for the Brown
Burmese, although a slight fading of eye colour is permitted.

CHOCOLATE BURMESE (CHAMPAGNE BURMESE)

Chocolate is another modification of the gene for black (ie Brown in the
Burmese) and is accepted as a separate breed by the GCCF and several
American bodies. The overall colour of the adult should be a warm milk
chocolate. The ears and mask may be slightly lighter but the legs, tail and
lower jaw should be the same colour as the back. Evenness of overall colour

CHOCOLATE BURMESE

is looked for. The nose leather should be warm chocolate brown and the foot pads a brick-pink shading to chocolate. In other respects the cat should be as the Brown Burmese.

LILAC BURMESE (PLATINUM BURMESE)

Lilac coats have been produced by mating two Chocolate Burmese which also carry a blue factor or a Chocolate with the blue factor to a Blue. Those kittens which acquire the Chocolate modification plus a double dose of Blue have the Lilac (Platinum) coat which in maturity should be a pale, delicate dove-grey to which a slightly pinkish cast gives a rather faded effect. The ears and mask can be slightly darker in colour. The nose leather should be lavender-pink. The foot pads are shell-pink in kittens and become lavender-pink as they become adult. In all other respects the Lilac should be as the Brown Burmese. They are recognized as a breed in Britain and can be registered in the CCA.

RED BURMESE

Red colouring in the Burmese was first achieved through matings involving a Red Tabby and a Red-pointed Siamese. The colour is now accepted as a breed in Britain. The coat should be a light tangerine. At present slight tabby markings are permitted on the face and small indeterminate markings

LILAC BURMESE

RED BURMESE

elsewhere (except on the sides and belly) if the cat is otherwise a good specimen. The ears should be distinctly darker than the back. The nose leather and foot pads should be pink. In other respects this breed should be as the Brown Burmese.

TORTOISESHELL BURMESE

The Tortoiseshell coat, a female-only colouration, appeared in the same breeding programme as the Red. Although the colour and markings are not considered so important in shows as adherence to the Burmese type, the coat should be a mixture of brown, cream and red without any obvious barring. The coat may display two shades of its basic colours and thus appear to display three or even four colours which may be mingled or blotched. Blazes, solid legs and solid tails are all permissible. The nose leather and foot pads may be plain or blotched, brown and pink. In other respects this cat, recognized as a breed in Britain, should be as the Brown Burmese.

CREAM BURMESE

Cream was produced in the same breeding programme as the two previous types. As with the Tortie, slight tabby markings may be found on the face and small indeterminate markings are permitted elsewhere (except on the sides and belly) in otherwise excellent cats. The coat should be a rich cream with ears only slightly darker than the back coat colour. Nose leather and foot pads should be pink. In other respects this cat, recognized as a breed in Britain, should be as the Brown Burmese.

BLUE-CREAM BURMESE

Another product of the breeding programme for coloured Burmese, this female-only type, recognized as a breed in Britain, should be a mixture of blue and cream, without any obvious barring, which may be distributed as freely as in the Tortie Burmese. Colour and markings are not deemed so important as type. Nose, leather and foot pads may be plain or blotched blue and pink. In other respects this breed should be as the Brown Burmese. Illustrated on page 112.

CHOCOLATE TORTIE BURMESE

Further selective breeding has produced this British-recognized breed which should be a mixture of chocolate and cream without any obvious barring and distributed as for the Tortie Burmese. Burmese type is more important than colour and markings. Nose leather and foot pads can be plain or blotched, chocolate and pink. Illustrated on page 112.

TORTOISESHELL BURMESE

CREAM BURMESE

BLUE-CREAM BURMESE

CHOCOLATE TORTIE BURMESE

112

LILAC TORTIE BURMESE

LILAC TORTIE (LILAC CREAM) BURMESE

Yet another Tortie variation of the Burmese, recognized as a breed in Britain. The lilac and cream mixture, distributed as for the Tortie Burmese, should have no obvious barring. Burmese type is more important than colour and markings. Nose leather and foot pads can be plain or blotched, lilac and pink.

SIAMESE CATS

The cat world has many legends about the origin of the various breeds and charming fables to explain their individual characteristics but even what appear to be straightforward historical reports often have no evidence to support them. It has often been said that the first Siamese Cat to be seen in Britain (some versions say it was a pair) was brought from Siam in 1884 by Owen Gould, the British Consul General in Bangkok. It was supposed to have been given to him by the King of Siam. Either this cat, or another imported one, was exhibited by his sister at the Crystal Palace in the following year. During the next few years more of the type appeared and the first Standard of points was published in *Our Cats* in 1892. Some writers give as little credibility to the Thai court origins of the Siamese as to the geographical origins of the Abyssinian or the Russian Blue, pointing out that Siamese types have occurred in other countries and that they,

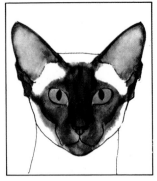

The Siamese head should be wedge shaped narrowing in straight lines to a fine muzzle

or cats remarkably like them, appeared in Western art several centuries earlier. The German naturalist and explorer, Peter Pallas, described and published a picture of a cat, which he saw when exploring around the Caspian Sea in 1794, that had a light chestnut brown body and black markings very like the points of a Siamese. It was born of a black cat and may have been just one of many natural mutations occurring from time to time. However a picture of the Seal Point, or Vichien Mas as it is called, appears in a set of pictures and verses made probably 400 years ago in the Ayudha period of Siam.

Whether or not the Siamese owes its development to the kings of Siam, it is generally accepted that it is of Eastern origin. It has been suggested that the Siamese is a partially albinic variation from the Burmese Cat and one Victorian expert declared that it was "derived from a cross between the Sacred Cat of Burmah and the Annamite Cats that were introduced into the religiously sealed and guarded Burmese and Cambodian Empire of Khmer..." Perhaps one day someone will produce some firm evidence to engage our belief in one theory or another — meanwhile Siamese owners may believe whatever they like.

The first Siamese cats bred in Britain looked very different from the breed that is admired today. They were much heavier in build and had comparatively rounded heads, and were not that different in type from the British Short-hairs. But by 1902 when the first Standard was established they were already described as "in every particular the reverse of the ideal short-haired cat" and were admired for their "svelte" appearance. But they often had squint eyes and kinked tails — both faults in the opinion of today's breeders. These characteristics led to picturesque stories about their origins: the kink had been acquired because the cats of an oriental princess wore her rings upon their tails while she went bathing, and bent the ends to keep them on, or they had curled their tails around a temple chalice they were set to guard and gained their crossed eyes from watching it so carefully.

The modern Siamese is expected to have a wedge-shaped head with a smooth outline both in profile and frontal views. There should be no pinching in of the cheeks, nor any roundness either, although there may

114

be a change of angle at the top of the nose. Cats with the "old-fashioned" more rounded head would stand little chance on the show bench but can still be very beautiful cats.

It is not only their elegant appearance which makes the Siamese the most popular of the pedigree breeds. They have a character and temperament which sets them apart. Usually very intelligent, they take more easily to a lead than most cats and can be very resourceful in learning tricks and inventing games. Equally, they can be efficient thieves and cunning in getting their own way. They become very attached to their owners and like to be involved in everything that is going on, demanding attention all the time and showing considerable jealousy if attention is directed away from them. They can be extremely talkative and sometimes stridently insistent. Some Siamese have a harsh voice which can be irritating and when in season almost all Siamese queens have a loud and penetrating call which can be heard at a considerable distance.

When first introduced, the Siamese was considered to be a delicate cat, susceptible to disease, but if it comes of healthy stock a Siamese kitten is as fit as any other, will usually develop more rapidly than other breeds and will already be displaying an assured and adventurous personality when only a month old. They mature physically very early and a female may begin to call when only six months old (a kitten calling at four months is not unknown); some males are capable of reproduction when not very much older, although they will certainly not have finished growing. The Siamese seem to be a particularly randy breed but they should not be mated at such an early age. They usually have largish litters of four, five or more kittens.

SEAL POINT SIAMESE

Siamese cats range widely from very large males to diminutive females but the Standard calls for a medium-sized cat with a long, svelte body and slim legs with small oval feet. The hind legs should be slightly longer than the front ones. The long, thin tail, which should not be thick at the base, tapers to a point. It can be either straight or, in Britain, may be very slightly kinked — though the kink should only be felt and must not be visible. The head should be long and well proportioned with width between the eyes. It should narrow in perfectly straight lines to a fine muzzle, with a straight profile, strong chin and level bite. The ears should be rather large, pricked, wide at the base and pointed at the tip. The eyes should be oriental in shape and slanting. They should be a clear, deep blue. The coat is short, fine and sleek and lies very close to the body. In winter it may grow a little longer.

The pattern of markings is rigidly defined and should be restricted to the mask and points, which must be clearly distinguished, and a darker shading of the coat on the shoulders and the rump. In most cats the coat darkens considerably all over as they get older and the points may develop brindling if the cat is ill or off colour, or during very hot weather. The face mask should spread out from the nose and eyes over the cheeks and chin but the darker colour should not run down over the throat. Delicate pencillings of mask colour link with the ears but there must not be any sign of a complete hood. The ears, tail, legs and feet should all be densely coloured. Often cats have a dark smudge on the belly but this would be a fault, for the underside and chest should be very pale and without any darker hairs. Any white patches on the feet would disqualify a cat from showing, as would pale "spectacles" around the eyes.

The Seal Point was at first the only variety of Siamese Cat to be recognized, although other colours did occasionally appear and a number of others are now recognized.

In the Seal Point the body colour should be cream shading into a pale warm fawn on the back and showing no sign of greyness. The mask and other points should be seal brown — a really dark brown — and the pads and nose leather should be the same colour as the points. In fact the Seal Point is theoretically a "Black Point" for it is genetically black. However, the genetic dilution which produces the characteristic points also weakens their colour to produce the deep "seal" tone.

Kittens are almost white when born and have a rather fluffy coat with no trace of markings. The first sign of the points appears as a smudge around the nose. Only then is it possible to tell what colour variety the kitten will be if the parents carry the genes for more than one variety. The points become more sharply defined as the cat gets older but the pencilling between the mask and ears may not develop until the cat is fully adult and this is allowed for by judges when kittens are being shown.

BLUE POINT SIAMESE

The Blue Point was the second variety of Siamese to gain recognition. The first cat is said to have been registered in 1894 and they were appearing in both British and American shows by the 1920s. They should have all the characteristics of the Seal Point except for colour which should be a glacial white, shading into light blue on the back. The points should be a darker blue which should be a cold colour but not the slate grey or gunmetal shade which appears in many specimens.

Blue Points have a reputation for being more gentle and less temperamental than the Seal Point Siamese but they still prefer plenty of human attention and will not like being left alone for long periods.

CHOCOLATE POINT SIAMESE

Chocolate-pointed cats appeared among the earliest Siamese to be bred in Britain but they were generally considered to be poorly coloured Seals although their colouration is due to a distinctly different gene. Gradually

SEAL POINT SIAMESE

BLUE POINT SIAMESE

interest in them grew but it was not until 1950 that they were recognized as a breed by the GCCF. In the years following they were accepted by all the North American registration bodies. The Standard is the same as for the Seal Point except that the coat should be ivory in colour; any shading should be the colour of the points – milk chocolate and all of the same density with the ears no darker than the other points. Good Chocolates are difficult to breed because cross breeding with Blue Points to produce the Lilac Point Siamese inevitably introduced Blue into the Chocolate strains and a colder tone has appeared in their coats than was the case before about 1960. Chocolate-to-Chocolate matings will sometimes produce more Lilac than Chocolate kittens when parents carry blue. The kittens develop their colour more slowly than the Seal and Blue Point and young kittens with a complete mask will probably be too dark when they mature, indeed a Chocolate may not reach full coloration until it is well over a year old. The colour fluctuation effected by sun and temperature changes in all Siamese is especially noticeable in the Chocolate Point.

LILAC POINT (FROST POINT) SIAMESE

Originally known as the Frost Point, although most associations now call it the Lilac Point, this breed occurs when both parents carry the recessive genes for Chocolate *and* Blue. The Lilac offspring will breed true. They follow the Standard for Seal Point Siamese except in colour which should be a glacial off-white (Magnolia) with shading, if any, to tone with the points which should be pinkish grey according to the British requirements. According to associations in America, the Lilac Points coat should be milk white or glacial white, with points of frost-grey with a pinkish tint. In Britain the nose leather and pads are described as faded lilac. The American Cat Fanciers Association ask for nose leather to be a translucent old lilac with paw pads of a cold pink and the Cat Fanciers Association requires both nose leather and pads to be lilac-pink. In North America the eyes of all Lilac Points should be deep or brilliant blue while in Britain a "clear, light vivid blue (but not pale)" is specified.

RED POINT SIAMESE (RED COLORPOINT SHORT-HAIR)

This breed, begun by mating Seal Point females with Red Tabby Short-hair males, took many years to develop as breeders had difficulty in keeping a good Siamese type. Recognition in America came in 1956 but they were at first known as Red Point Short-hairs, although most associations now accept them as a variety of Siamese. British breeders had to wait another 10 years before the GCCF gave recognition. Many of the early cats showed shadow tabby markings and not until the Tabby Point had been developed were they allowed to be called Red Point Siamese. The prevalence of the tabby pattern with red cats and the effect of the colour restriction factor

CHOCOLATE POINT SIAMESE

LILAC POINT (FROST POINT) SIAMESE

on the colour strength has tended to lead to the development of cats with very pale masks and points. The sought-after effect is a white coat with shading (if any) to apricot on the back; mask, ears and tail a bright reddish-gold and legs and feet bright reddish-gold or apricot. The nose leather should be pink and the eyes a bright vivid blue. At present barring and striping on the mask, legs and tail are not deemed faults under the British Standard. In other respects the Red Point should be as the Seal Point Siamese.

TORTIE POINT SIAMESE (TORTIE COLORPOINT SHORT-HAIR)

Like all Tortoiseshell cats these are considered to be a females-only variety. They can be produced when a Seal Point is mated to a Red Point or from a Tortie Point mating with any of the other Siamese types. They were first developed by crossing Red and Tortoiseshell Short-hairs with Siamese in an attempt to produce Red Point colouring. Tortie Points conform to the basic Seal Point Siamese type other than in colour which consists of a mingling or patching of red and/or cream with the basic colour of either Seal, Blue, Chocolate or Lilac types. The colour is naturally restricted to the mask and points but the distribution of the patching is random and immaterial on points and leathers although barring and ticking are deemed faults. Nose leather and eyes should be as in the equivalent solid colour Siamese. Some of the American registration bodies do not class these highly individual looking cats as Siamese but group them with the Colorpoint Short-hairs.

TABBY POINT SIAMESE (LYNX POINT SIAMESE, TABBY COLOR-POINT SHORT-HAIR)

Examples of this colouration were recorded at the very beginning of this century and were seen for a time in the mid-forties, when they were given the unofficial name of Silver Point Siamese. It was not until the sixties that they began to attract attention. They were recognized in Britain in 1966 as Tabby Point Siamese, although at times they were previously known as Shadow Points, Attabiys and Lynx Points — the name by which they are known by some registration bodies in North America, Australia and New Zealand. Other American associations classify them with the Tortie and Red Points as Colorpoint Short-hairs.

In Britain the Tabby variation of the basic Seal, Blue, Chocolate and Lilac Siamese colours and of all the Tortoiseshell variations of these colours are grouped together in this breed. On the European Continent some bodies recognize each as a different breed but the basic requirements are the same. The type is as for the Seal Point Siamese. The body should have a pale coat, free from markings and conforming to the basic colour standard for the particular colour of points. The legs should have broken horizontal stripes of varying size with the back of the hind legs solid. In Tortie Tabby Points there should be some mingled red and/or cream patching on the legs. The tail should have clearly defined rings of varying size and end in a

RED POINT SIAMESE (RED COLORPOINT SHORT-HAIR)

TORTIE POINT SIAMESE (TORTIE COLORPOINT SHORT-HAIR)

121

solid colour tip. The mask should have clear tabby stripes, especially around the eyes and nose, with dark rimming or toning to match the points on the eyelids and darkly spotted whisker pads. The ears should be solid colour with no stripes but with a "thumbmark" on the back, except in the Tortie Tabby Points when they should be mottled red and/or cream. Nose leather and pads should conform to the basic colour Standard or the nose may be pink. The pads of Tortie Tabby Points should be mottled. The eyes should be a brilliant clear blue.

Tabby Point Siamese have all the qualities of the Siamese family. Some breeders suggest that they have gentler characters than the typical Seal Point but they are usually very confident individuals.

The Red Tabby Point Siamese is not recognized within this breed by the GCCF — it is visually indistinguishable from the Red Point and only by its progeny can it be established whether it is Tabby or self-colour if it is born of Tabby Point parentage.

CREAM POINT SIAMESE

The Cream Point and Cream Tabby Point versions of the Siamese type are visually indistinguishable since both will carry tabby markings. They follow Siamese type in every way. The body colour should be a warm white and the legs and face a shade like that of clotted cream while the ears, nose and tail should be a pale warm apricot and the nose leather and pads pink. The Cream Point Siamese would be grouped under Any Other Dilution Siamese in Britain, a group introduced to allow for possible colour variations not recognized as separate Siamese breeds.

ALBINO SIAMESE

This variety, known in America, but not recognized elsewhere, is genetically a true albino and shows no pigmentation having a white coat, pink skin and a pink undertone to the eyes.

COLORPOINT SHORT-HAIR

Some breed registration bodies do not recognize the Tabby Point (Lynx Point), Red Point and Tortoiseshell Point Siamese as true Siamese and classify them as Colorpoint Short-hairs. They are illustrated and described under the Siamese classification.

TONKINESE

A rare variety, so far recognized only by the Independent Cat Federation and not given breed status outside America, which was first produced by crossing Siamese and Burmese. Similar cats have been bred in Britain.

TABBY POINT SIAMESE (LYNX POINT SIAMESE, TABBY
COLORPOINT SHORT-HAIR)

CREAM POINT SIAMESE

123

FOREIGN WHITE

This is *not* the same cat as the American Albino Siamese, although this British breed of extreme foreign type is a cat in which the genetic factors restricting the colours to the Siamese points have been so dominant that there is no trace of them in the coat. There were problems with deafness in the development of the breed and although those strains were discontinued many veterinarians are still unconvinced that many of these cats do not have an inherent weakness to a number of diseases.

The Foreign White is a lightly built, long and lissom cat with fine proportions and a graceful appearance. The head should be long and wedge-shaped in profile and the face should narrow in straight lines to a fine muzzle. The eyes should be clear brilliant blue and oriental in set; the ears wide at the base, large and pricked. The legs should be long and slender with small, neat oval paws and the tail should be long, tapering and whiplike. The coat should be completely white and the paw and nose leather pink.

HAVANA (HAVANA BROWN)

The Havana is a Chocolate Siamese cat in which the dilution factor which produces the points of the Siamese does not operate, although American breeders have developed it away from the original and both the CFA and CFF now penalize a Siamese head. The breed was developed by British breeders who first exported Havana kittens to the United States in 1956. Two years later the GCCF recognized the breed but refused the name Havana lest it confuse the origin of the cat and it became known as the Chesnut Brown (Foreign) Short-hair. In America it is known as the Havana Brown and in 1970 the British body agreed to revert to the original name of Havana.

The British Standard calls for a cat of Foreign type which is fine in bone, lithe, sinuous and of graceful proportions with a long body, slim, dainty legs with neat oval paws and the hind legs slightly higher than the front legs, and a long whip tail with no kink. The head should be long and well proportioned, narrowing to a fine muzzle, with large pricked ears which are wide at the base and set well apart. The eyes should be slanting and oriental in shape and decidedly green in colour. The American Standards require a less extremely Foreign type, eyes that are oval in shape and slightly rounded ear tips. They also specify that the head should have a distinct stop at the eyes when seen in profile and a whisker break.

The short glossy coat should be even throughout and a rich chestnut brown in colour. Some cats have a melanistic tendency which is a fault and most will lose colour here and there during a hot summer, the tail tip bleaching to a gingery colour; they should obviously not be shown at that time of year.

British breeders found that continued breeding of like-to-like in the early days of the breed led to loss of stamina, yellowing of eye colour and a darker coat. They corrected this by crossing out to Siamese Chocolate

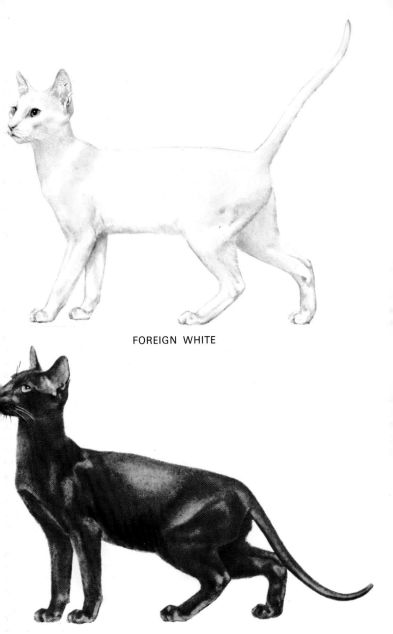

FOREIGN WHITE

HAVANA (HAVANA BROWN)

Points which have helped to maintain the extreme Foreign type which is required in Britain.

This is an extrovert and healthy breed which breeders have found does not have the digestive difficulties with milk so frequent in Siamese. It is however, somewhat susceptible to cold and damp.

FOREIGN LILAC (FOREIGN LAVENDER)

This self-coloured cat can be produced only when both parents carry the genes for blue and chocolate. Some fine examples appeared during the breeding of the Havana but it was not until the end of the 1960s that breeders began to develop it as a distinct type. It is accepted by some registration bodies in the United States and will no doubt soon become a fully recognized breed. In effect a self-coloured Siamese, it should have a soft and glossy coat which is frost-grey in colour with a pinkish tone. The head should be long and well proportioned, narrowing in straight lines to a fine muzzle and a strong chin. The ears should be large, pricked and set well apart. The oriental eyes should be a rich green, although kittens may show a tinge of blue or yellow. Paw pads should be pink. The ACFA standard asks for a slightly heavier cat than the Siamese.

EGYPTIAN MAU

This breed is a conscious attempt to recreate a cat like the ones which appear in the sculptures and paintings of ancient Egypt. In America it was developed from cats which actually came from Cairo in 1953 and in Britain it had its origin in tabbies of foreign type which were produced during the breeding of the Tabby Point Siamese. The Mau (the Egyptian word for cat) is recognized by a number of American registration bodies in Silver (sloe-black markings on a pale silver ground) and Bronze (dark-brown markings contrasting with a light-bronze ground) and is approaching recognition in Britain in several tabby colours.

The British cat has the extreme Foreign type of its Siamese ancestry with oriental eyes, but in America a less Foreign type is required and although the eyes should be oval and slanting, fully oriental eyes are a fault. The CFF standard specifies an Abyssinian type head. The eye colour should be green, yellow or hazel. The American cat must have a spotted coat pattern but in Britain mackerel tabby markings are also allowed. A charming refinement in the British cat is the insistence on a special mark in the form of a scarab beetle between the ears which recalls the amulets of the pharaohs.

OCICAT

A breed developed in the United States from the crossing of a Chocolate Point Siamese male and a half-Siamese, half-Abyssinian female which has not yet achieved Championship status and is so far unknown in Britain

FOREIGN LILAC (FOREIGN LAVENDER)

EGYPTIAN MAU

and scarcely known on the European Continent. They have short silky fur patterned with spots and with tabby markings on the throat, legs and tail and golden eyes. Two colour varieties have been produced, both with pale cream fur. The Dark Chestnut has dark chestnut brown spotting and bars and the Light Chestnut has milk chocolate coloured markings. They are rather similar to the Egyptian Mau.

KORAT

There is no dispute over the origin of the Korat. Whatever the arguments may be about the origin of the Siamese, this is a cat which quite definitely comes from Thailand where it is called the Si-Sawat and has been known for centuries. Occasional specimens have appeared in the West but the breed was not really known outside Siam until a pair were taken to America in 1959. They were accepted as a distinct variety in 1966 and are now also becoming known in Europe.

This is a medium-sized, strong and muscular cat with a fairly low-lying body and a rounded line to the back. The medium-length tail is heavy at the base and tapers to a rounded tip. The face is appealingly heart-shaped with plenty of space between the disproportionately large eyes, a large flat forehead and a well-developed but not sharply pointed muzzle. There is a slight stop between forehead and nose, and in males there is a depression in the centre of the forehead. The ears are large with rounded tips.

The Korat's close-lying coat is a silvery-blue unlike that of any other breed, without white spots or markings even in the kitten coat. An old Siamese poem describes the fur as "smooth with roots like clouds and tips like silver." The nose leather, lips and paw pads are dark blue or lavender and the pads may have a pinkish tinge. The blue eyes of the kitten become first amber and then a dazzling green-gold. In Thailand the Korat is considered a lucky cat (Sawat means good fortune or prosperity) and is highly prized by the people of the Korat Plateau. According to Jean L. Johnson, who during six years in Thailand was unable to buy one, they were "given only to the highest officials as a taken of esteem and affection." Eventually friends managed to obtain a breeding pair which were sent to Mrs Johnson after she had returned to America where they began the Western strain. In their homeland the males are known as great fighters but they also make good fathers and happily share their lives with their queen and kittens. They can be much less tolerant of cats not so closely related. In the home they have a quiet and intelligent disposition, wanting to participate in whatever is going on. But they do not like sudden loud noise and cats for the show bench should be accustomed to noise and disturbance when kittens or they will be very nervous on exhibition.

JAPANESE BOBTAIL

Although only recently introduced to the United States and still almost unknown in Europe this is an ancient breed which has been known for

KORAT

JAPANESE BOBTAIL

129

centuries in Japan. The Gotokuji temple in Tokyo is decorated with row upon row of pictures of one of these cats called Maneki-Neko. Every one shows its paw raised in a gesture of greeting which has become a symbol of good luck and each is a portrait of this distinctive breed which also appears in many famous Japanese paintings and prints.

The Japanese Bobtail is not like any other kind of cat. It neither fits into the foreign nor the domestic body type, for although sturdily built and well muscled it is comparatively slender. The back legs are longer than the fore legs but if the cat is relaxed they are usually kept bent so that the back remains on an even level. The tail is short and carried curved so that although its full length may be 4 or 5 it appears to be only 2 or 3 inches long; long hair grows in all directions giving a bobtail effect like that of a rabbit.

The breed has no connection with the Manx or the Stumpies which Manx matings frequently produce and it does not carry the lethal gene which can affect the entire vertebral column of the Manx. The head should form a perfect equilateral triangle with gently curving sides, high cheek bones, a long nose and big ears. The big, oval eyes are set on the slant. The soft and silky coat is traditionally tri-coloured (black, red and white) but the Cat Fanciers Association provisional standard accepts a wide variety of colours including solid, bi-coloured and tortoiseshell but the pattern must be sharply marked with distinctly separated patches and Siamese points or unpatterned agouti are not allowed. The coat sheds less than most other breeds.

CORNISH REX

The Rex cat has an unusual kind of fur which originally appeared by accidental mutation. The first recorded was born some time before 1946 in East Berlin but the history of the Cornish Rex begins with a kitten born in Cornwall, of a tortoiseshell-and-white farm cat and an unknown father, in 1950. The rest of the litter had straight coats but this one had a curly coat. Litters sired by this cat were half curly-coated and in 1957 two Rex-coated kittens were taken to the United States. In 1959 an American example of Rex mutation appeared in Oregon and from 1959 a number of kittens bred from the German strain during the 1950s were imported. No pure American strain was established. There is no evidence to show that the American mutation is genetically compatible with any other. Cornish and German Rex have, however, been successfully cross-bred and are probably genetically identical. Both Cornish and Devon Rex were given British breed recognition in 1967 but only one type is recognized in America.

In most cats the coat is made up of four kinds of hair: guard hairs, which are long, straight, thick and evenly tapered; awn hairs, which curve from the root and thicken before abruptly tapering; awned down hairs, a crimped intermediate between the previous two; and down hairs, which are evenly thin and crimped. There are nearly 50 times as many down hairs as guard hairs. In the Rex coat there are only down hairs, or a combination of awned down hairs and down hairs in the case of the German Rex. The hair length is about half that of normal cats and its thickness about 60 per cent of normal. This gives a short plushy coat which should curl, wave or ripple, particularly on the back and tail. Whiskers and eyebrows should be crinkled and of good length. Any coat colours are acceptable but white markings must be symmetrical, except in the Tortoiseshell-and-White.

The body should be hard and muscular, slender and of medium length, with long, straight legs and small oval paws. The head has a medium wedge shape with the length about one-third greater than the maximum width, narrowing to a strong chin. The skull should be flat and in profile a straight line should be seen from the centre of the forehead to the nose. The ears are large and set high. They are wide at the base, taper to rounded tips and are well covered with fine fur. The tail is long, fine and tapering and also covered with curly fur. The oval eyes, of medium size, should be of a colour in keeping with the coat colour.

DEVON REX

In 1960 a Rex-coated kitten was born in Devon which, when mated with a Cornish Rex female, produced only plain coated kittens. It was genetically different. Second generation matings – in which the Cornish and Devon

CORNISH REX and head of DEVON REX

genes were mixed — produced a Rex type. In Britain it was accepted as a separate breed in 1967 and has since been recognized elsewhere except by some American bodies.

Like the Cornish Rex, this breed had its origins in a mutation from a British type domestic cat — yet Rex all seem to show a Foreign type body. The British Standard specifies a broad chest and slender neck, and unlike the Cornish there should be full cheeks and a strongly marked break to the nose. The muzzle is short with a strong chin and a whisker break and the forehead curves back to the flat skull. The eyes are large, oval shaped, slanting towards the outer edges of the ears, and wide set; the colour should be in keeping with the coat colour or (except when the Rex carries Siamese points, when it is known as the Si-Rex) be chartreuse, green or yellow. The Devon coat, which feels harsher than the other Rex, should be short and fine, wavy and soft. Whiskers and eyebrows should be crinkled and of medium length.

GERMAN REX

A strain which can be traced to a black female born in East Berlin before 1946 from which a planned breeding programme produced curly-coated cats from the 1950s and which contributed to the development of the Rex in the United States. German Rex possess a combination of down hairs and awned down hairs but have no guard hairs. It is probably genetically identical to the Cornish Rex.

EXOTIC SHORT-HAIR

This cat, recognized as a breed by the Cat Fanciers Association in 1967, is a deliberately created hybrid which has the body type usual for the long-haired Persian cats but wears a short coat of fur. The most usual cross has been between a pedigree Persian long-haired cat and an American Short-hair but Burmese have been used with equal success since the American Standard for Burmese requires a less foreign cat than that of Europe and its rounded head, broad chest and compact body contribute towards the sought-after Exotic type.

The Exotic is a large and robust cat but quality is much more important than size. In appearance it is ideally a top quality Persian with the exception that instead of the long, flowing coat of the Persian it has a unique coat of short (medium by Short-hair standards) fur which is soft, resilient and dense. The body is short and cobby, well supported by short sturdy legs. It should be deep in the chest and equally massive across the shoulders and rump, well-rounded in the middle and with a level back The tail is short and thick but in proportion to the body length. The round massive head is set upon a short, thick neck and has small, round-tipped ears which tilt forward, broad jaws, full cheeks, a broad snub nose and large round eyes set well apart.

EXOTIC SHORT-HAIR

All the Persian colours and patterns recognized in North America are permitted except for the Peke-Faced Red.

American Short-hair cats with a little Persian blood in their background, which fitted the Standards for the Exotic, were for a time allowed to transfer to this breed, although they had been previously registered as Short-hairs. They are the only cats which have been permitted to retain wins made under a previous category.

LONG-HAIRED CATS

Long-haired cats were unknown in Europe until the end of the 16th century when, it has been claimed, a French scientist and archaeologist called Nicholas Fabri de Peiresc brought back a long-haired cat from Turkey.

Although cats imported from Turkey, and from Persia, seem to have been highly prized as rarities, it was not until nearly 300 years later — at about the time of the Crystal Palace Cat Show of 1871, when pedigree records began to be kept and planned breeding undertaken — that they began to be seen in any numbers in the West. The cat fanciers of the late 19th century preferred the Persian type to the more wedge-shaped head of the Turkish Angora cat and the name Persian became synonymous with long-haired cat. Today, with the exception of the Angora, which has been revived as a separate breed, and a handful of others, the show cats in the long-haired group are expected to conform to the same basic requirements. Long-haired cats is now the official British name for this group but many people still refer to them as Persians and in America the name is still officially used for Long-hairs other than the Angora, Balinese, Birman, Himalayan, Maine Coon and Turkish cats and some recently created breeds.

All the cats of the Persian group should have cobby bodies (which means long and low lying) set upon short thick legs. The head should be round and broad with full cheeks, a short, almost snub, nose and a distinct break between the nose and the skull, known as a stop. The ears should be small, neat and spaced well apart and the eyes should be round and large. The tail should be short and thick. The coat should be long and silky, with no sign of woolliness. The head should be framed by a ruff of longer hair which is brushed up and away from the body and neck to make it more noticeable on show cats. It continues as a deep frill between the front legs. There should be long tufts of hair on the ears and the tail should be very full with a greater bush of hair at the tip than at the root.

Long hair of the kind shown in domestic breeds does not exist in any of the wild members of the cat family. Although cats like the Northern Lynx and the Snow Leopard have longer hair than cats of warmer lands, they obtain protection from cold by having thicker rather than longer fur, and in particular a much thicker undercoat. It seems likely that long hair in the domestic cat has developed from mutant types and that domestication has made its continuance possible, for it would be a handicap rather than an asset to the wild cat.

The breeders of long-haired cats have sought to produce an even more flowing and luxuriant coat and this demands help to keep it in good condition and free from matts and burrs. Even if the original ancestors of our modern Long-hairs could keep their own coats in good condition, the domestic Long-hair of today should have at least one, and preferably two, thorough brushings every day. The effort is rewarded by the attractiveness of the glossy, silky coat of the well-cared for cat.

ANGORA

At one time all the long-haired cats in the West were known as Angora cats for it was from the city of Angora, or Ankara as we know it today, that the first long-haired cats seen in Europe were thought to come. The Turkish capital has also given its name to the goat from which the long silky wool we call mohair comes and, by transference, to the Angora rabbit. It has often been suggested that the Turkish origin of the long hair is as mythical as some of the other legends explaining the development of the various breeds, but Angora cats certainly existed in Turkey and were a distinctly different type from the "Persian" cat which later became the standard for the usual long-haired breeds. The Angora has a longer body and tail than the Persian type and its head is smaller with upright ears. It had been supplanted by the heavier cat in Europe and America and was in danger of becoming extinct in Turkey until the Ankara Zoo began a carefully controlled and recorded breeding programme to ensure their survival.

In 1963 the Governor of Ankara gave permission for a pair from the Zoo

ANGORA

to be taken to the United States. One was a white female with amber eyes the other an odd-eyed white male. From this pair and another, with the eyes reversed, which was taken to America three years later, the breed has been re-established in the United States and, since they bred true, it was recognized by the Cat Fanciers Association in 1970. It is not recognized in Britain.

The Angora should be of small to medium size, the male being slightly larger than the female. It is fine-boned with long legs which are slightly higher at the rear so that the rump is carried high. It has a sturdy body but is longer and more lithe than the Persian and has a longer, tapering tail. The head is small to medium size, wide between the long pointed ears and tapering towards the chin. The nose is longer than the Persian type and has no break. The eyes are large and slightly almond-shaped with a slight slant. Only white cats are recognized in the United States although there is no reason why other colours should not appear. The fine coat is medium long and silky soft with a good ruff, a full tail and tufts on the ears and between the toes. It has a tendency to waviness, especially on the stomach. Pads and nose leather should be pink. Eyes may be blue, amber or odd-eyed but, as with other whites, blue-eyed cats are likely to be deaf.

TURKISH

This is another cat which has been domesticated for many centuries in Turkey. It did not appear in Europe until 1955 when a pair were given to an English breeder travelling in Turkey who decided to take them home and eventually to establish the breed in the West. This was no easy task as, in order to enlarge her breeding stock, she had to return to Turkey to find new cats which then had to spend months in quarantine on arrival in Britain. In 1969 they were recognized by the GCCF.

The cats were known initially as Van Cats because they originally came from the locality of Lake Van in south-eastern Turkey but Turkish Cat is now the official name in the Cat Fancy. In many ways they are similar to the Angora. The body is long but sturdy with tail and legs of medium length and neat round feet with well-tufted toes. Males should be particularly muscular on the neck and shoulders. The head should be shaped like a short wedge with well-feathered, large, upright ears which are set fairly close together and a long nose.

The fur should be long, soft and silky to the roots with a woolly under-coat and a full tail. The main colour should be a chalk white with no trace of yellow but with auburn markings on the face, which should have a white blaze, and an auburn tail with faint darker auburn rings in adults and more distinct ring markings in kittens. The ears should be white, the nose tip, paw pads and the inside of the ears a delicate shell pink.

The Turkish cat has also earned the name of Swimming Cat for the breed not only swims (most cats can if they have to) but actually enjoys being in the water. They will even enjoy being bathed if the water is kept to a temperature around 101°F (38°C) which is their own blood temperature.

TURKISH

Unless it is a really hot sunny day, when they can safely dry off in the sun, they should be rapidly and thoroughly dried with warm towels if they have been in water and should not be allowed to lie about when wet. All cats will attempt to lick themselves dry but towelling and a gentle brushing in front of a fire will prevent any risk of a chill and enhance the appearance of their coat. However, these are hardy cats. In their native region around Lake Van there is snow for six months of the year. They make affectionate and intelligent pets but since litters are small it will be some time before they are easy to obtain.

MAINE COON CAT

There is no truth in the story that this breed is the result of matings between racoons and the domestic cats of the early American settlers: such a coupling is biologically impossible. It probably had its origin in uncontrolled crosses between American domestic cats and Angoras or other long-haired cats brought from the East by the sailors of New England. It was well known right through the eastern states and was often seen in shows at the turn of the century but interest in the breed waned for about 50 years until the establishment of the central Maine Cat Club in 1953. The club holds shows exclusively for Maine Coon Cats in May each year at Skowhegan. Coon cats can be quite large, weighing as much as 30 pounds, but they have a reputation for being shy.

They should be muscular but have the small to medium tapering head and the long-legged, long-bodied look of the Angora with large ears and large, slightly slanting eyes. The cheek bones should be set high and the chin firm and in line with the upper lip and nose, which should have little or no break. Both a short flat face or an over-long nose would be counted as faults. The fur is not as long as in Persian cats nor is there as full a ruff. It is short on the front shoulders increasing in length towards the tail, which is tapering but blunt-ended. It is longish on the stomach and on the haunches, where it forms a heavy pair of breeches. The Maine Coon Cat can be any colour or pattern and the eyes may be green or as appropriate to the coat colour. The fur is easier to keep in condition than that of the other Long-hairs.

BROWN TABBY LONG-HAIR (BROWN TABBY PERSIAN)

The tabby is such a basic pattern in the cat that, as with its short-haired cousin, there are many domestic pets with a brown tabby coat but few of them would match the exacting requirements of the show bench. Although once a very popular breed, pedigree cats are not often seen today and there are not many breeders specializing in this cat. They can be extremely attractive and have the reputation of being hardy, intelligent and affectionate.

The present colour, which breeders describe as a rich tawny sable, was introduced at the end of the last century and provides a fine contrast with the dense black markings. The body should be massive and cobby, like all cats of Persian type, with short legs, a short tail and a broad, round head with well-placed and well-tufted ears, a short broad nose and full round cheeks. The eyes should be large, round and hazel or copper in colour. The long flowing coat and full tail should have well-defined markings. The British Standard specifies delicate black pencillings running down the face, two or three distinct swirls crossing the cheeks, two unbroken narrow lines crossing the chest, butterfly markings on the shoulders, regular stripes on the front legs from the toes upwards, deep bands running down the saddle and sides and regular rings on the tail. The black markings should be a little narrower than the ground colour between. The British Standard makes no reference to the oval "oyster" whorls on the sides or to striping, and both the classic and mackerel patterns are grouped in the same class, but in the United States the two patterns are shown in separate classes.

Because the Brown Tabby Long-hair does not attract the attention of a great many breeders there are not many pedigree strains and it may prove difficult to find a suitable stud for like-to-like matings. Silver Tabbies should not be used for this may weaken the rich sable colour and make the eyes yellowy-green. Red Tabbies will not improve the stock either. If a Brown Tabby is not available a Black or dark Blue of good type will probably give the best results. Some breeders mate to Blue and back to Brown Tabby to improve and produce fine markings. Avoid any cat with a white lip or chin – although a lighter colouring here is permissible – since this is one of the most difficult faults to eradicate.

MAINE COON CAT

BROWN TABBY LONG-HAIR

BLUE TABBY PERSIAN

Tabbies with a blue coat have from time to time appeared naturally in Brown Tabby litters and can also be produced by a Brown Tabby with a Solid Blue, although this does not usually result in such a fine coat as in like-to-like matings. It is not recognized as a breed in Britain and is still rare in the United States although it has been accepted in America since 1962.

The type should be as for all Persians and the colouring, as specified in the Standard, should be a pale bluish ivory (including the lips and chin) with markings in a very deep blue which makes a dramatic contrast. Overall there should be a warm fawn overtone. Nose leather should be "old-rose" and the paw pads rose-coloured. The large round eyes should be a brilliant copper.

SILVER TABBY LONG-HAIR (SILVER TABBY PERSIAN)

At its best this is an extremely beautiful cat but, although they have been known since the earliest days of the Cat Fancy, they are difficult to produce with both good type and fine markings. They should be of full Persian type with cobby bodies and short thick legs, a short tail and a broad round head with a short nose, wide muzzle and small, well-tufted ears that are set well apart. The big round eyes should be green or hazel. The coat should be long, dense and silky in texture with an extra long frill. The ground colour should be a pure pale silver with decided jet black markings. Any bronze tinge or brindling is a fault. Kittens which carry clear tabby markings at birth do not usually mature into well-marked cats. Those which are born nearly black at birth with markings only on the legs and sides, developing their full pattern when about 4 to 6 months old, often prove to be the most handsome cats.

BLUE TABBY PERSIAN

SILVER TABBY LONG-HAIR

141

RED TABBY LONG-HAIR (RED TABBY PERSIAN)

The Red Tabby of 70 years ago was a bright golden red and before that might have been more accurately described as an Orange Cat; today the required colour is a deep rich red. It should have the cobby, solid body and short thick legs of the typical Persian with a broad round head, full cheeks, short nose and small well-tufted ears. The coat should be long, dense and silky with the tail short and flowing with no white at the tip. The eyes should be large and round and a deep copper colour. The tabby markings may be either marbled or mackerel and in North America there is a separate show class for each pattern. As with other tabbies, the American Standards go into great details and the markings on the head and neck should meet the butterfly pattern on the shoulders. Many people believe this is a male-only breed. This is not true.

CREAM TABBY PERSIAN

This is a North American breed, no Cream Tabby Long-hair being recognized by the British and European Fancies. Cream, genetically a dilute form of red, does not make it easy to get a clear contrast between the ground colour, which should be a very pale cream (including the lips and chin which must not be white) and the markings which should be buff or cream of sufficient depth to be clearly differentiated but still stay within the dilute range. Both the marbled and mackerel forms of marking are recognized and a separate class is held for each in shows. The nose and paw leather should be pink and the large round eyes should be brilliant copper.

RED SELF LONG-HAIR (SOLID RED PERSIAN)

The Red Self, or Solid Red as it is more usually called in America, was originally known as the Orange Persian and the coat colour is indeed more of a deep orange than a scarlet red. Few perfect coats are seen for tabby markings frequently persist, especially on the face and tail. A dearth of Red Self females has prevented the development of like-to-like breeding in recent years but breeding from Tortoiseshell females with Red Self males (which will give Black and Red Self males and Tortoiseshell or Red Self females) or from Blue-Cream females with Red Self males with no blue in their genetic formula (giving the same results) should lead to the development of Red-to-Red breeding stock.

The Red Self should conform to the usual requirements for long-haired cats and should have deep copper eyes. The ideal is a rich red coat which is sound and unmarked. Illustrated on page 145.

RED TABBY LONG-HAIR

CREAM TABBY PERSIAN

143

PEKE-FACED

The Peke-Faced cat is not recognized in Britain but it was already contesting championships in the United States over 40 years ago. It was developed from Red Self and Red Tabby Long-hairs which showed heavy jowls and gains its name from the similarity of its face to that of the Pekinese Dog, which it should resemble as closely as possible. The forehead must be high and bulge over the nose to form a sharp stop. The nose is so short that it appears depressed or even indented between the eyes and in profile it is hidden by the cheeks. The muzzle should be wrinkled and a fold of skin runs from the inner corner of each eye to the outer edges of the mouth. The ears are large and prominent and the eyes large and round. Both Red and Red Tabby-coated varieties are recognized in America. As with the Pekinese Dog, breeding for this facial type can cause problems. Emphasis on the short nose can lead to breathing difficulties and the teeth of the upper and lower jaw do not always meet correctly. The fold of skin beneath the eyes can also cause the tear ducts to become blocked. Breeders have to take great care to avoid the perpetuation of deformities and the deliberate development of such an extreme appearance with these inherent dangers has attracted considerable criticism from veterinarians.

Peke-Faced cats should conform to the standards for their Red and Red-Tabby relatives in all respects other than the head and neck. Kittens do not always show the full facial characteristics until they are several months old.

CHINCHILLA (SILVER PERSIAN)

The first Chinchilla is said to have been created by an English breeder in the 1880s from a cross between a Silver Tabby and a Smoke but the cat of the last century was much darker than that exhibited today and showed clear tabby barring on the legs which would now be a fault. Chinchillas, or Silvers as they are called by some bodies in North America, are almost always born quite dark and with tabby markings, especially on the tail. These disappear as they grow older and a fine adult specimen should have a pure white undercoat and the end of each hair of the back, flanks, head, ears and tail should be tipped with black giving a sparkling silver appearance. The legs can be very slightly shaded with the tipping but the chin, ear tufts, stomach and chest must be pure white. There should be no tinge of brown or cream and no tabby markings. The tip of the nose should be brick-red, the paw pads and the visible skin on the eyelids black or dark brown giving a sharp, eye-liner effect around the large, round and most expressive eyes which should be emerald or blue-green in colour.

The silky coat should be fine, dense and long — especially long on the frill. The Chinchilla should have the cobby head and short thick legs of the Persian type with a broad round head having a broad muzzle, snub nose, small, wide-apart ears, which should be well tufted, and a short bushy tail.

RED SELF LONG-HAIR

PEKE-FACED

The Chinchilla is usually smaller than other Long-hairs and is almost always a more fine-boned and dainty looking cat than the rest of the Persian type. This is expected of the breed in Britain but in America it is required to meet the same standard as the more heavily built breeds and is at a disadvantage in competition although that has not prevented Silvers from carrying off top awards.

SHADED SILVER PERSIAN

No longer recognized in Britain, where it was dropped in 1902 because judges could not distinguish between it and the early Chinchillas, this is still a well-loved breed in North America and is also recognized elsewhere, including Australia. It is not easy to distinguish Chinchilla and Shaded Silver kittens when they appear in the same litter — some of the darkest kittens turn out to be Chinchillas although the Shaded Silver is the darker adult. The Shaded Silver coat might be described as a pewter look when compared with the silver of the Chinchilla. The undercoat should be white, and the mantle — the name given in the American Standard for the shaded area covering the sides, back, flanks, head, ears and tail — should have each hair tipped with black (considerably more heavily than in the Chinchilla) grading from dark on the ridge to white on the chin, chest and stomach and under the tail. The legs should match the tone of the face. Nose leather should be brick-red and the paw pads black. The visible skin which rims the eyes should also be black and the lips and nose should be outlined in black. The eyes should be large, round and green or blue-green. The conformation is as for the Chinchilla.

MASKED SILVER PERSIAN

This breed, recognized by some organizations but not by the GCCF, is a Chinchilla in all respects except that the face is masked in a very dark colour and the paws are also dark.

BLUE CHINCHILLA

Not yet given breed recognition, this is in all respects the same as the Chinchilla except that the fur of the mantle of the coat is tipped with blue-grey instead of black giving a very ethereal effect.

CHINCHILLA

SHADED SILVER PERSIAN

SHELL CAMEO

Cats with a pink coat have appeared from time to time in uncontrolled matings but today's Cameo Cats owe their existence on the American show bench to carefully planned breeding during the 1950s and were first recognized as a breed in the United States in 1960. They have not yet achieved breed status in Britain. This red cat with a silver undercoat has been produced from crossings between Chinchillas and Solid Reds. One of the reasons for their slow development in Britain is the lack of good Red Selfs and in Britain, Creams (cream being a dilute of red) have been used but cream-tipped cats are not acceptable in America.

The overall type is that of other Long-hairs but good colouring is of greater importance to breeders. The Shell, which is the palest of the Cameos should have an undercoat of ivory white, according to the American Standard. In Britain it should be off-white to very light cream. Each hair of the mantle extending over the back, flanks, head, ears and tail should be lightly tipped with red. In Britain the Shell may have light cream tipping instead of red. The face and legs may be lightly shaded but the chin, ear tufts, stomach and chest and underside of the tail should be without any ticking at all and there should be no sign of any barring. The nose leather, pads and eye rims should be rose-coloured. The eyes should be a rich copper colour. One of the difficulties of using Chinchillas in developing this breed lies in the persistence of the green eye colour. For this reason Smoke cats have been used instead but they do not produce such a fine lustrous coat as the Chinchilla.

SHADED CAMEO

This is a darker form of the Shell Cameo with the same white undercoat and chin, ear tufts, stomach, chest and underside to the tail while the mantle should be evenly ticked with red. Leather and eye rims should be rose-coloured and the eyes deep copper.

SMOKE CAMEO (RED SMOKE)

The darkest of the Cameos, this is identical to the Shell and Shaded Cameos in type and distribution of colour but the ticking is so strong that it appears to be an all-red (or perhaps all-cream in Britain) when it is lying still, but in movement the pale undercoat is revealed and creates an effect of rippling pink. The Smoke Cameo (called the Red Smoke in America by the Cat Fanciers Association) is variously described by the different Standards as having an undercoat of white, ivory-white, or ivory to light cream and, as with the other Cameos, both Red and Cream ticking of the mantle are possible in Britain. Eyes should be copper and leather and eye rims rose-coloured. Illustrated on page 151.

148

SHELL CAMEO

TORTOISESHELL CAMEO

TABBY CAMEO

Although Tabby markings are a fault in the other Cameo breeds, a Cameo Tabby coat is recognized in the Exotic Short-hair and by some associations for American Short-hairs and Persians.

TORTOISESHELL CAMEO

A tortoiseshell-patterned Cameo is recognized by most of the American registration bodies. The Standard requires a silvery white undercoat with ticking of both black or blue and red or cream to produce a pattern resembling the standard Tortoiseshell. Except for colour it should be the same as the other Cameo breeds.

BLACK LONG-HAIR (BLACK PERSIAN)

The Black Long-hair is probably the oldest of the pedigree long-haired breeds. Harrison Weir, organizer of the first great British cat show in 1871, described it as both "the most sought after and the most difficult to obtain." A pure black is difficult to find for a single white hair will show against the coat and under certain lights most black cats will reveal faint bars and stripes on their body or legs which would be a serious fault in a show cat. However, a kitten showing grey or rusty fur or even with a sprinkling of white hairs may well grow up to be a perfect black cat, indeed some of the densest black adults start off a very bad colour and do not begin to achieve a good coat until they are 6 months old. Often they will not look their best until in their second coat at 12 or 18 months old.

In addition to its lustrous raven black hair, the Black Long-hair should have large, round and wide-open eyes of copper or deep orange. The eyes must not have any trace of green, a fault which breeders find very hard to eradicate.

Both sunshine and damp can affect the colour of the coat, long periods of sunbathing or even excessive licking resulting in a brownish tinge, which may also appear during moult.

Most breeders believe that Black Long-hair stock can be improved by occasional cross-breeding with Blue Long-hairs, and many champions have a Blue Long-hair not far back in their pedigree. The introduction of too much Blue blood will lead to a lightening of the coat. Males from a Blue-Black mating are not usually used in pedigree breeding. Blacks can be used in the breeding of Tortoiseshells, Calicos, Whites and Bi-colours.

Black Long-hairs require considerable grooming before a show. Powder or dry shampoo will mar the coat if it is not completely removed and some exhibitors bathe their cats with a suitable soap or shampoo about a week before a show. Grooming with a silk handkerchief or a pad of chamois leather will develop the sheen on the coat and may help remove any stray white hairs since these are usually of a coarser texture than the rest of the fur.

SMOKE CAMEO (RED SMOKE)

BLACK LONG-HAIR (BLACK PERSIAN)

BLUE LONG-HAIR (BLUE PERSIAN)

The Blue must conform to the general long-hair requirements and have copper-coloured eyes, but any shade of blue is allowed for the coat provided that it has an overall even hue. Lighter shades are frequently preferred and this is included in the American Standard, although a darker shade which is sound at the roots is more acceptable than an unsound lighter shade. The Canadian Standard both prefers lightness of shade, provided that the cat conforms to type, and requires a short snub nose with a clear break.

At one time most cats exhibited a frill that was lighter than the rest of the coat and this was so difficult to avoid that the British Standard included a note encouraging members to show their cats even if they did not fully match up to the Standard. Careful breeding has now raised standards and this advice no longer applies.

Blue Long-hairs are often used to improve the type and eye colour of other Long-hairs and they are a vital factor in the breeding of Blue Cream Long-hairs. Blue kittens often have tabby markings when they are born, especially on the legs, but these soon disappear as the fur grows and a heavily marked kitten may become the most perfectly coated adult. Blue kittens with lovely pale coats sometimes occur in White Long-hair litters.

BLUE-EYED WHITE LONG-HAIR (BLUE-EYED WHITE PERSIAN)

This breed must have pure white fur with deep sapphire-blue eyes. It has developed from the Angoras which were the first Long-hair cats taken to Europe and many cats have a longer nose, narrower head, taller ears and longer body than is desirable in a modern Long-hair. The eye colour is also difficult to achieve as kittens with blue eyes may well have green ones when adult, or even develop one green eye and one blue one. Matings between perfect-eyed cats are no guarantee of correct colour in the litter.

Blue-eyed Whites usually have small litters and their kittens are often delicate. There was a decline in numbers until the introduction of Blue Long-hairs and Odd- and Orange-eyed White into breeding programmes in recent years.

White long-haired cats with blue eyes are almost always deaf. There appears to be a genetic link between the eye colour and a pathological change in the cochlea in white cats, but if a kitten has the slightest smudge of dark colour, even one which disappears as it grows older, the cat is likely to be unaffected. This deafness factor has encouraged the use of other eye colours in breeding. Deaf-to-deaf breeding should be avoided. Cases have been reported of blue-eyed cats born deaf gaining their hearing during kittenhood and this may be very frightening for the cat until it has got used to its newly acquired sense.

White cats usually keep themselves very clean but feet and paws cannot avoid getting soiled and may require washing in warm soapy water in preparation for a show. Yellow markings caused by grease can be disfiguring and males especially may require extra grooming and powdering to remove it.

BLUE LONG-HAIR (BLUE PERSIAN)

ORANGE-EYED WHITE LONG-HAIR with (inset) BLUE-EYED and ODD-EYED variations

ORANGE-EYED WHITE LONG-HAIR (COPPER-EYED WHITE PERSIAN)

The Orange-eyed variety of the White Long-hair developed when the Blue-eyed type was mated with Long-hairs of other colours with orange eyes. Both eye colours were shown in the same classes but the Orange-eyed cats almost always proved to be of better Long-hair type and were recognized as a separate breed in Britain in 1938. In North America they were already treated as a separate variety at the end of the last century.

Orange-eyed cats are free of the deafness factor which affects Blue-eyed White Long-hairs and the eye colour is more predictable. Cats of this type can result from matings with other colours which may produce mixed litters and crosses with Blue Long-hairs are often made to improve a strain. (Illustrated on page 153)

ODD-EYED WHITE LONG-HAIR (ODD-EYED WHITE PERSIAN)

Although recognized as a breed and given a breed number by the GCCF in 1968, the Odd-eyed White cannot achieve Championship status in Britain, but in America it has been fully recognized since the early 1950s.

With the exception of one or two isolated instances, white cats appear to be the only colour in which the phenomenon of different coloured eyes in the same cat occurs. They appear in litters of both Blue-eyed and Orange-eyed cats and are extremely valuable to breeders of Blue-eyed White because they do not carry the deafness factor, although it has been claimed that they may be deaf on the side of the blue eye. (Illustrated on page 153)

CREAM LONG-HAIR (CREAM PERSIAN)

The Cream Long-hair is said to have evolved from matings between Blues and Reds, but it is also possible that it may have developed from very pale Reds. At one time it was known as the Fawn Persian and was much darker than is acceptable today when the Standard requires that it should be a pale to medium cream (many are too "hot", that is too ruddy) which is pure and sound throughout without any shading or markings. Like all Persian types, the body should be solid and cobby and set on thick legs. The broad round head should have a short broad nose, broad round cheeks and small, well-set ears. The large round eyes should be deep copper in colour and the coat long, dense and silky with the tail short and flowing. The fur tends to darken slightly before moulting and regular brushing is necessary to remove it and to keep the coat looking a clear cream colour.

There tend to be more male Creams than females. If a Blue male is mated to a Blue Cream the litter may include Cream and Blue males but the females will be Blues and Blue Creams. Female Creams can only be produced by

CREAM LONG-HAIR (CREAM PERSIAN)

mating Cream males to Cream or Blue Cream females or by mating Red Self male carrying blue to Tortoiseshell females carrying blue and by mating Red Self males carrying blue to Cream and Blue Cream females.

BLUE CREAM LONG-HAIR (BLUE CREAM PERSIAN)

This breed, produced originally from Blue and Cream matings, is often of outstandingly good type as the two contributing breeds are known for their close adherence to the requirements for Long-hair type. The dense soft and silky coat should consist of pastel shades of blue and cream softly intermingled to conform to the British Standard giving an effect rather like shot silk. There should be no clearly defined patches of either colour. In North America exactly the opposite is required. The blue and cream should be clearly separated into well-defined patches and intermingling is a fault. A good American Blue Cream is blue with patches of solid cream distributed over body, tail, legs and face. In practice, cats with cream on at least three feet, with chins half cream and half blue and with noses and foreheads of differing colour are preferred. A cream blaze running down from the forehead is particularly liked. On both sides of the Atlantic the eyes should be large and round and deep copper or dark orange in colour.

Blue Creams are almost always female and the rare males are invariably sterile. The colouring can appear in Tortoiseshell litters as well as in Blue and Cream matings. A Blue Cream female mated to a Cream may produce Blue Cream females, Blue males, and Creams of both sixes. Mated to a Blue, the litter may include Blue Cream females, Cream males and both male and female Blues.

SMOKE LONG-HAIR (BLACK SMOKE PERSIAN)

The origin of the Smoke is uncertain but it was known more than a century ago and then thought to be the result of chance matings between Blacks, Whites and Blues; another theory suggests that it had its origin in the Chinchilla. Described in the British Standard as a "cat of contrasts", the undercolour should be "as ash-white as possible, with the tips shading to black, the dark points being most defined on the back, head and feet, and the light points on frill, flanks and ear-tufts." The body is cobby and massive, but not coarse, with short legs, a short bushy tail and a broad round head with a snub nose and small tufted ears which are set well apart. The large round eyes should be orange or copper in colour. The long, dense, silky coat should be black on the back shading to silver on the sides, flanks and mask. The feet should be black with no markings. The extra-long frill and ear tufts should be silver. When the adult cat is in movement the white undercoat should be seen clearly. The kittens are born black or blue and the undercoat does not begin to show until they are about three weeks old. In young adulthood the tips of the hair may lighten and the roots become darker but the second adult coat comes through with a clearly defined black top-coat, mask and legs, silver frill, ear-tufts and chest and an undercoat as white as possible. Frequent grooming is necessary to prevent old hair obscuring the undercoat and to enable it to show through the dense black.

BLUE SMOKE LONG-HAIR (BLUE SMOKE PERSIAN)

The Blue Smoke owes its origin to Smoke-Blue matings and should be identical to the Smoke except that where the tipping of the Smoke is black it should be blue in this variety. The same clear contrast between colours should be apparent and the eyes should be orange or copper coloured.

BLUE CREAM LONG-HAIR (BLUE CREAM PERSIAN)

SMOKE LONG-HAIR (BLACK SMOKE PERSIAN)

BI-COLOURED LONG-HAIR (PARTI-COLOURED PERSIAN)

Bi-coloured, or Parti-coloured cats, as they are sometimes known in America, were given recognition with championship status in 1966 in Britain and are recognized by the Cat Fanciers Association in America, but are not yet accepted by all the other bodies. At first the British Standard required a cat to be marked like the Dutch rabbit but, as with its short-haired cousin, the Standard for the long-haired Bi-Colour was amended in 1971 to allow a much less formal distribution of pattern. Like all Persian types, this breed should have a massive cobby body — indeed the Bi-colour is usually a big cat — set on short thick legs with a short tail. The head is round and broad with width between the ears which should be small, well placed and tufted. The nose should be short and broad and the cheeks full. The muzzle should be wide and the chin firm with a level bite. The large round eyes should be deep orange and set well apart. The coat should be of a silky texture and long and flowing with extra length on the frill and tail.

The Bi-Colour's coat, according to the present British Standard, may be "any solid colour and white, the patches of colour to be clear, even and well distributed. Not more than two-thirds of the cat's coat to be coloured and not more than a half to be white. Face to be patched with colour and white."

TORTOISESHELL LONG-HAIR (TORTOISESHELL PERSIAN)

Tri-coloured cats have appeared from random matings for centuries but they are not an easy cat to produce to order. As Tortoiseshells are almost always female and the rare males born invariably sterile, like-to-like breeding is not possible, and crosses are usually with one of the Self colours which make up the coat. A Tortoiseshell mother may produce several litters and not have a single kitten like herself and to attempt to produce a Tortoiseshell by cross-breeding cats of its component colours has even less chance of success. The long-haired Tortoiseshells that do exist include a great many with tabby markings or other faults which would make them unsuitable for showing.

The body should be cobby and massive, like all Long-hairs, with short legs, and a broad round head with full round cheeks, a short broad nose and small well-tufted and well-placed ears. The large round eyes should be deep orange or copper. The coat should be long and flowing with extra length on the frill and brush. Both British and American Standards require that the coat should have the three colours — black, red, and cream — well broken into patches and the colours should be bright and rich. Brindling, white hairs and tabby markings are all undesirable and black should not be the predominant colour. The colours should be well broken on the face and a cream or red blaze running from nose to forehead is especially liked.

BI-COLOURED LONG-HAIR (PARTI-COLOURED PERSIAN)

TORTOISESHELL LONG-HAIR (TORTOISESHELL PERSIAN)

TORTOISESHELL-AND-WHITE LONG-HAIR (CALICO PERSIAN)

The Tortoiseshell-and-White Long-hair, also known in North America as the Calico cat, has the colour patching of the Tortoiseshell interspersed with white but the Standards vary from association to association. The British requirement is for black, red and cream, interspersed with white and well-distributed, but in North America the Cat Fanciers Association specifies a white cat with unbrindled patches of black and red, white to be predominant on the under parts. The National Cat Fanciers Association accept "Black and red and/or cream in clearly defined and well-broken patches" and the American Cat Fanciers Association give this detailed description: "The head, back, sides and tail should be black, red, and cream in clearly defined and well-broken patches. The Tortoiseshell-and-White pattern should resemble a Tortoiseshell cat that has been dropped in a pail of milk. The feet, legs, the whole underside and half way up the sides of the body should be white. The "milk" should have splashed up on the nose and half way around the neck." The breed should have the long flowing coat, cobby body and broad round head of the Persian type and the large round eyes should be orange or copper in colour.

BLUE TORTOISESHELL-AND-WHITE LONG-HAIR

Tortoiseshell-and-White Long-hairs mated with Blue-and-White Bi-coloured males have produced a Blue Tortoiseshell-and-White, but this attractively coloured cat has not yet received recognition and no official Standard has been issued.

BROWN LONG-HAIR

This experimental variety has not yet been recognized as a breed but was first produced in 1961 by crossing an Havana with a Blue Long-hair. It is of full Persian type with a rich chestnut-brown coat which changes to a tawny colour immediately prior to moulting. The eyes may be copper to orange in colour.

LILAC LONG-HAIR

Another variety which is still awaiting recognition, this typical long-haired cat is a somewhat brownish Lilac and has orange eyes.

SEAL COLOURPOINT (SEAL HIMALAYAN)

Random matings have from time to time produced Siamese cats with longer than normal hair and controlled breeding in Sweden in the 1920s, America in the early 1930s and in Britain just before World War II, attempted to

TORTOISESHELL-AND-WHITE LONG-HAIR
(CALICO PERSIAN)

SEAL COLOURPOINT (SEAL HIMALAYAN)

create a strain which would combine the Persian type with Siamese colouring. However, breeders did not succeed in establishing a new variety. Most of the cats created were long-haired Siamese and it was not until the end of the 1940s that real progress was made in transferring the Siamese points to a Persian type.

Mating long-haired cats with Siamese produces kittens which are unlike either parent: they are short-haired and self-coloured, these features being genetically dominant, nevertheless, they carry the genes for long coats and the Siamese pattern which appear together in about one in sixteen of subsequent matings. To achieve a Persian type either outcrossing to other Long-hairs is necessary — the method used in Britain — or a selection of the closest to the desired type in the "half-way" Himalayans may be used in a carefully controlled breeding programme. The latter method was mainly used by American breeders.

By 1955 the breed was at last sufficiently well established in Britain for the GCCF to recognize the Seal and Blue Point varieties under the name Colourpoint (the use of Black and Blue Long-hairs to produce the type accounted for these colours being recognized first). In 1957 the breed was first given recognition in America, but under the name Himalayan. The American and British Standards are very similar, demanding a cat of Persian type with a cobby body, low head with a short face and short nose with a distinct break or stop, well-developed cheeks and small tufted ears with width between them. Any similarity in *type* to the Siamese, in particular a long straight nose, is considered most undesirable and incorrect.

The fur should be long, thick and soft in texture with a full frill. The body colour of the Seal Point should be cream with seal-brown points as in the Seal Point Siamese. The large round eyes should be a brilliant blue. The nose leather and paw pads of all Himalayans should be in keeping with the points colour.

BLUE COLOURPOINT (BLUE POINT HIMALAYAN)

First given recognition in 1955, at the same time as the Seal Colourpoint, this breed is like it in all respects except colour which should be a glacial white on the body with blue points as in the Blue Point Siamese. In both Seal and Blue Colourpoints, the body colour of the coat may darken a little after the second adult moult.

CHOCOLATE COLOURPOINT (CHOCOLATE POINT HIMALAYAN)

The Chocolate Point is identical to other Colourpoints except that the points should be the warm chocolate colour of the Chocolate Point Siamese and the body colour ivory with any shading on the body toning in with the points. To produce this colouration outcrosses to both Chocolate Point Siamese and Havana Brown Short Hairs were used.

162

BLUE COLOURPOINT (BLUE POINT HIMALAYAN)

CHOCOLATE COLOURPOINT (CHOCOLATE POINT HIMALAYAN)

LILAC COLOURPOINT (LILAC OR FROST POINT HIMALAYAN)

LILAC COLOURPOINT (LILAC OR FROST POINT HIMALAYAN)

Lilac was the next Colourpoint colour to be produced, combining the genes for chocolate with those for blue. The body of the coat should be a magnolia colour with the Lilac shade restricted to the points as in the other colour varieties. In both the Lilac and Chocolate Colourpoints the pale body colour usually stays throughout the cat's life and their fur does not show the darkening with age characteristic of the other colours.

RED COLOURPOINT (RED POINT HIMALAYAN)

The Red Colourpoint should be identical to the other colour varieties except that the body should be off-white and the mask and points a well-defined red. Cream Colourpoints (the dilute form of red) have now been produced but have not yet been given a British Standard.

TORTIE COLOURPOINT (TORTIE POINT HIMALAYAN)

The body colour of the Tortie Colourpoint should be cream. In other respects it is identical to the other colour varieties except that the British Standard apparently limits the mixed colouring to the mask for it specifies the "points colour of Tortie Points to be restricted to the basic Seal colour, body shading, if any, to tone with points."

RED COLOURPOINT (RED POINT HIMALAYAN)

TORTIE COLOURPOINT (TORTIE POINT HIMALAYAN)

SEAL POINT BALINESE

The Balinese is actually a Siamese cat with longer hair. It was developed by American breeders who discovered that mutant kittens with longer coats than usual which appeared in Siamese litters bred true when mated. Breeders of normal Siamese objected to their being called long-haired Siamese since Siamese implies the complete look of the oriental cat and they were first recognized under the name Balinese in 1963. They were introduced to Britain in 1974. In all respects except the length of fur, which should be two inches or more, they should follow the Siamese type. They should be svelte-looking cats, elegant but muscular in build. The long head should be of medium size and taper in a wedge shape from the nose, flaring out in straight lines to the large pointed ears to form a triangle, and with no break at the whiskers. The eyes should be medium-sized, almond-shaped and slant towards the nose. Neck and legs are long and slender, the hind legs set higher than the front. The paws should be small and oval, the tail long and thin, tapering to a point.

The coat should be fine and silky and an even tone all over contrasting with the dense and clearly-defined mask and points which should be without brindling or white hairs. The mask should cover the whole face, including the whisker pads, but should not extend over the top of the head although it should be connected with the ears by tracings. In the Seal Point Balinese the body colour should be a warm pale fawn to cream, shading to a lighter tone on the chest and stomach. The points, mask and nose leather should be a rich seal brown. The eyes should be a deep vivid blue.

BLUE POINT BALINESE

Identical to the Seal Point Balinese in all but colour, the Blue Point should have a coat of cold-toned bluish-white which shades to white on the chest and stomach. The points should be deep blue and the nose leather and paw pads slate. The eyes should be the vivid blue of the true Siamese. Balinese do not have the ruff of the usual long-haired cat.

CHOCOLATE POINT BALINESE

The same Standard applies to the Chocolate Point as to the other varieties of Balinese except that its body colour should be ivory with no shading, the points a warm-toned milk chocolate and the nose leather and pads cinnamon-pink. The eyes should be a deep vivid blue. Balinese have the powerful voice of the Siamese but are reputed to be less demanding of their owners. Illustrated on page 169.

SEAL POINT BALINESE

BLUE POINT BALINESE

LILAC (FROST) POINT BALINESE

The Lilac Point is identical to the other Balinese varieties except that its body should be glacial white with no shading, and the points and mask should be a slightly pinkish frosty-grey. The nose leather and paw pads should be lavender-pink and the eyes a deep vivid blue. The coats of most Balinese tend to darken as they grow older but there should still be a very clear contrast between the body colour and the points.

SEAL POINT BIRMAN

This intriguing breed was recognized in France in 1925 but was not introduced to Britain and the United States until the middle of the 1960s, receiving recognition from the GCCF in 1966 and from the Cat Fanciers Association in America in 1967. The breed was supposed to have been introduced to France in 1919 when the priests of a temple in Indo-China sent a pair as a present to two soldiers who had come to their assistance during a rebellion. One of these cats died on the journey but the other, a female, was pregnant and the breed was established in France. This breed is also known as the Sacred Cat of Burma and is supposed to be the type of cat which was kept in temples centuries ago. According to a legend current in cat circles, if not in Khmer history, there was a white cat at the Temple of Lao-Tsun in the days before the coming of Gautama Buddha which would accompany the chief priest in the worship of the blue-eyed, golden goddess Tsun-Kyan-Kse. Their country was invaded and one night as the priests gathered before the goddess to ask her for guidance and protection the chief priest died. As his spirit left him the cat leaped upon his head and the assembled monks saw its fur change colour to the gold of the goddess and its eyes to dazzling sapphire blue while its ears and paws became the colour of the fertile earth except for where they rested on the old man's silver hair. The spirit of the old man had passed into the cat and the goddess had given the cat her own clear colours. The cat turned from the goddess to face the entrance to the temple beyond which soldiers could be heard approaching. Given courage by this manifestation of the goddess the monks repelled the invaders and saved the temple. Later the other temple cats took on her sacred colouring.

Whatever credence you may give that legend the Birman should have a creamy-gold coat (the British Standard describes it as beige which is slightly golden), bright blue eyes, a mask, tail and paws of rich seal brown and each paw tipped with white like a glove. The United States and Canadian Standards specify that the "gloves" on the front paws should end in an even line at the third joint and on the back paws should cover the entire paw ending in a point, called the laces, going up the back of the hock.

The body conformation is not like that of most long-haired cats. The Birman's body should be long and low on its short strong legs with a longish tail. The head should be wide, round and strongly built with full

CHOCOLATE POINT BALINESE

LILAC (FROST) POINT BALINESE

SEAL POINT BIRMAN

cheeks and slightly flat above the eyes. The North American Standards also require a Roman nose of medium length with low set nostrils. The fur should be long with a good full ruff and a bushy tail. It should have a silky texture and be slightly curled on the belly. Nose leather should match the seal colour of the points and paw pads should be pink.

BLUE POINT BIRMAN

The Blue Point colour variety should be exactly like the Seal Point Birman except that the mask, ears, tail and lower legs should be blue-grey and the nose leather slate. All Birman kittens are born with all-over pale coats and the darker points do not begin to develop until they are several weeks old.

CHOCOLATE POINT BIRMAN

All Birmans follow the same standard except in colour and the Chocolate Point, not yet recognized as a breed in Britain, should have points of warm milk chocolate with cinnamon-pink nose leather.

170

BLUE POINT BIRMAN

CHOCOLATE POINT BIRMAN

LILAC POINT BIRMAN

The Lilac Point Birman, which awaits recognition as a separate variety in Britain, should differ from other Birmans only in that its mask, ears, tail and lower legs should be frosty-grey and the nose leather should be lavender-pink. Birmans have a quiet voice and are very intelligent and affectionate.

RAGDOLLS

This unique breed, developed during the late 1960s in California, is now recognized by the National Cat Fanciers Association. In appearance Ragdolls are very like the Birman but with a heavier body, broader head and thicker fur, which the original breeder claims needs no brushing. Seal Point and Lilac Point varieties have been developed and either may have a slight white nose streak and white tail tip although this is not essential. They must, however, have the white mittens and boots of the Birman. Kittens are born white and do not obtain their full colour until they are about a year and a half old. Despite their colouring they are in no way related to the Siamese and have a very quiet voice.

The breed derives from a white Persian female which was very severely injured in a road accident. Apparently her offspring all have a unique disposition. They are extremely placid and physically so limp that they literally hang over your arm like a rag doll or bean bag. They appear to have lost all sense of danger and do not seem to feel pain which makes them extremely vulnerable. They are not geared to fight and are an easy prey for other animals which could kill a Ragdoll in a matter of minutes. They will lie down in the line of traffic and go to sleep. They are by no means fragile but must be kept away from strange animals, children that might hurt them and other dangers. Changes in behaviour or condition must be carefully watched for signs of ill health or injury. The Ragdoll has been described as "the closest one can get to a real live baby and have an animal" but its passive and dependent nature may seem to many cat lovers the very opposite of the feline characteristics that make a cat so attractive.

The breeding and sale of Ragdolls is carefully controlled by the International Ragdoll Cat Association who seek to provide a minimum price structure and limit the proximity of breeders.

SOMALI

For some years long-haired kittens have been appearing in Abyssinian litters in North America. Many breeders hid their existence to prevent damage to their reputations but now the attractiveness of these cats has won them recognition as a separate breed known in several American associations as the Somali. They are generally larger than the short-hair Abyssinian and appear in both its colour varieties: Red and Ruddy. The dense, fine-textured coat may be slightly shorter on the shoulders but ear tufts, breeches and a

LILAC POINT BIRMAN

SOMALI

173

full ruff are desirable. The eyes may be either green or gold but should be deep and rich in colour. In the Ruddy the nose leather should be tile-red and paw pads black or dark brown with black between the toes and running upwards on the hind legs. The Red has rose-pink nose leather and chocolate-brown pads and between the toes.

The Somali is an affectionate and lively cat with a quiet voice. The silky coat does not mat and requires only occasional combing, not the rigorous grooming needed by most long-hairs.

CYMRIC

Towards the end of the 1960s a number of long-haired kittens without tails appeared in Manx litters in the United States and from them this breed has been developed, although it has not yet been granted Championship status. Except for the hair length, the Cymric should follow the Standard for a good Manx in particular having no vestige of a tail and a definite hollow at the end of the backbone where the tail would normally begin. The hind-quarters should be high and the back short with good depth to the flank. The head should be large and round with a longish nose and very prominent cheeks. The ears should be wide and taper to a point. Coat may be any established colour or pattern with eye colour to match.

INDEX

Page numbers in italics refer to illustrations.